Five Operas and Richard Strauss

Five Operas and Richard Strauss

by Lotte Lehmann

translated from the German by
Ernst Pawel

The Macmillan Company, New York

The author gratefully acknowledges permission to include excerpts from operas by Richard Strauss:

Ariadne auf Naxos, copyright 1912, 1916, 1922 by Adolph Furstner; renewed 1940 by Furstner Ltd.; copyright assigned 1943 to Boosey & Hawkes Ltd. for all countries except Germany, Danzig, Italy, Portugal, and the U.S.S.R.; copyright renewed 1944 by Boosey & Hawkes Ltd.; reprinted by permission of Boosey & Hawkes Inc.

Arabella, copyright 1933 by Richard Strauss; renewed 1960 by Franz Strauss; reprinted by permission of Boosey & Hawkes Inc., Sole Agents.

Die Frau ohne Schatten (music by Richard Strauss; text by Hugo von Hofmannsthal), copyright 1916, 1919 by Adolph Furstner; renewed 1944, 1946; copyright assigned 1943 to Boosey & Hawkes Ltd. for all countries except Germany, Danzig, Italy, Portugal, and the U.S.S.R.; reprinted by permission of Boosey & Hawkes Inc.

First Printing

Printed in the United States of America

THE MACMILLAN COMPANY, NEW YORK

COLLIER-MACMILLAN CANADA LTD., TORONTO, ONTARIO

Library of Congress catalog card number: 64-17602

DESIGNED BY ANDREW P. ZUTIS

To my beloved Vienna Opera

Preface

JN OLD AGE, so they say, the past grows more vivid in the mind's eye. I may be old now, but I have not yet ceased to look ahead, to regard the future as ever promising and mysterious. And as for the past, it seems like a mere yesterday rather than a whole lifetime.

It lives on in me as though it were today.

But what I am talking about is not my personal past. Childhood, youth, marriage—how long ago it all seems. No, truly alive in me is but the one great and profound experience of my life—the stage. From out of the vast flow of memories there emerge moments such as are given to few artists— moments of triumph, of artistic growth, of dedicated work with masters whose very names have already become legend: Franz Schalk, Bruno Walter, Arturo Toscanini, Richard Strauss . . .

The last name makes me stop.

I had the rare good fortune to study with Strauss himself the operas which this book sets out to analyze. I sang them under his direction and know what he wanted. In one brief sentence or remark, he frequently gave me a clue or explanation that could prove of value to the generation of singers now coming of age.

It is my hope and wish that this book will be read in the spirit in which it was written, that is, not as a monument to personal vanity but as an attempt to do what I consider my duty: to pass on to others the heritage I received from a great artist.

Contents

Preface	vii
Ariadne auf Naxos	1
Ariadne auf Naxos—the Opera	13
Die Frau ohne Schatten	23
Intermezzo	71
Arabella	91
Arabella—the Opera	95
Der Rosenkavalier	119
Der Rosenkavalier—the Opera	123
Postscript	195
Second Postscript	199
Index	207

Five Operas and Richard Strauss

Ariadne auf Naxos

*T*HE YEAR 1916 was a rather important one in my life; I left the Hamburg Municipal Theater for what at that time still bore the proud name of "Royal and Imperial Court Opera" at Vienna. The clouds of war, however, already were casting long shadows over the once gay city, and the Emperor's throne, an expendable luxury item, was manifestly doomed. Thus I never really came to know the genuine glamour of Old Vienna about which I had heard so much—flower parades in the Prater or the procession of brightly resplendent carriages in the petal-covered Hauptallee. This, to me, was already part of the past, a glorious fairy tale; for the Vienna I came to know looked very different indeed. We lived in modest circumstances, with no more food than our regular ration cards entitled us to, and I still vividly remember suffering from acute hunger for the first time in my life. My rather substantial income proved of scant help in the matter, because what one needed in Vienna was "contacts"; we knew no one and had no access to the black market sources for butter, eggs, and milk. I shall never forget the kindness shown me by the singer

Richard Mayr. When I once confessed that I was hungry and simply did not know how to go about finding more than my allotted ration, he immediately began to have food sent to us regularly from his farm, and life brightened considerably. I have often blessed him for his generosity.

All in all, I felt rather out of place in Vienna, being myself terribly "German" in those days, utterly Prussian in my background and so alien to the natural geniality of the Viennese that I mistook for hypocrisy what I later learned to appreciate as a charming and graceful way of life. The Vienna Opera, too, was alien territory, and whereas in Hamburg I had been everybody's spoiled darling, in Vienna I was merely one among many—the New One, the "one from the sticks." Great stars reigned in solitary splendor among the soloists; there were Maria Jeritza, Selma Kurz, Lucy Weidt, Marie Gutheil-Schoder. And though I did have some gratifying success, I seemed to lack that certain extra which would put me in a class with the others. Franz Schalk, first conductor at that time and later the Opera's general manager, received a great many complaints about me, and I rather suspect that in those days he must have found me downright obnoxious, though we became good friends later on. At rehearsals he used to drop sarcastic remarks both about my musical abilities and my ill-mannered behavior toward my colleagues. I remember how one day our director, Wilhelm von Wymetal, took me aside to inquire if I could not possibly indulge my colleagues' hankering for somewhat more elaborate formalities. "For instance," he pointed out, "all you ever say is a simple *Good morning* instead of *Good morning, Frau Kammersängerin* [a title signifying Singer by appointment, to His Imperial and Royal Majesty]. Furthermore, what would it cost you to add a *How do you do?*" With devastating candor I replied that it would not cost me anything, but that I saw no reason for asking, since I really was not, after all, the least bit interested in how she was or was not doing. Wymetal had to laugh in spite of himself, wondering out loud what he was going to do with such an obstinate and confirmed Prussian.

Yet things did not always end in good-natured banter, and I was to discover time and again that a touch of charm and graceful diplomacy tends to oil the wheels and pay off in the long run.

Then a tense and expectant mood abruptly pervaded the Opera and gripped everyone at once: Strauss had written a new version of *Ariadne auf Naxos*, and the premiere was to take place in October. As a young novice in Hamburg I had sung the part of Echo in the old version; this time, however, I was assigned a splendid role—that of the Composer in the elaborate Prologue to the opera. Cause for great joy, of course, except for one minor detail—I was only the understudy. With tears in my eyes I worked on the part, lived myself into it, and somehow felt from the beginning that it had been written just for me, and for me only. But would I ever get the chance to prove it? All I had been asked to do was to be ready if for some reason Marie Gutheil-Schoder should cancel her appearance. And this, I knew, would never happen.

I found some crumbs of comfort in the fact that it was to be Gutheil-Schoder, at least, who would rob me of my glory, for I worshiped this great singing actress with all my heart. This made it a little easier for me to watch her create the role of the Composer, while I had to sit by and listen, rent by longing, dreams, and disappointment.

During one of the last rehearsals, I was suddenly summoned onstage; Frau Gutheil-Schoder had a cold and had been ordered to rest her voice. Strauss himself had announced that he would attend this very important rehearsal, and I was to sing the Composer, whose part extends throughout the entire Prologue, and who was therefore essential to the rehearsal.

Present along with Strauss were Hugo von Hofmannsthal,

Schalk, and Hans Gregor, the general manager. I felt no particular excitement, for, after all, I had merely been called in as a substitute for a single rehearsal, and no one would waste much attention on me. Carried away by the music, utterly living my role, I soon forgot my surroundings, and with my whole being plunged into the glorious experience of again creating a part. I forgot all about Strauss and about all the other very important onlookers. Instead, I was wholly transfigured into the Composer who, inspired by the beautiful legend of Ariadne, transmutes it by the genius of his imagination.

The legend itself is rather well known. Princess Ariadne saves bold Theseus from death by leading him out of the labyrinth inhabited by the man-eating monster. Theseus, grateful, sails with Ariadne to the island of Naxos, where he deserts her—God alone knows why. Ariadne was beautiful, young, and lovable, yet Theseus left her on this bleak island with only the spirits of the wind, the water, and the wild forest for company. Ariadne's grief resounded in the profoundly moving melodies created by the Composer—and I was the Composer, at least for the duration of that magic hour in which I was allowed to play his role.

The end of the rehearsal brought me back to reality. Strauss, whose presence I had all but forgotten, asked me to meet him that same afternoon for a rehearsal at the Opera. Flattered and surprised, I felt my heart beating wildly when I arrived for this fateful rehearsal, and the fact that both Schalk and Gregor also had turned up did not exactly calm my nerves.

When the rehearsal was over, Strauss simply declared that I was to sing at the premiere.

A Strauss premiere . . . Precisely the thing that had been missing from my career in Vienna. I was, of course, overwhelmed at the thought of being given a chance to create the very role which seemed as though it had been written for me.

Yet at the same time I was terribly upset that so great an artist as Gutheil-Schoder should be hurt on my account, no matter how blameless I was in actual fact. Gregor in his memoirs recounts this particular scene and with much humor stresses the point that this marked the first time in his life that he ever saw one soprano turn down a role out of consideration for another soprano.

I have no desire to assume any halo, and must therefore confess that I did capitulate with alacrity and even a measure of enthusiasm when told by the three gentlemen present that this happened to be strictly their business and that I was to do as I was told.

The fact that I, the New One, had the audacity to upset the hierarchy of established privilege did not contribute to my popularity among my colleagues at the Opera. It gave rise to much bitterness and consternation, including even a delegation sent to protest to the manager. Gregor, an old hand in the theater and wise to its ways, found this sudden spurt of uncommon solidarity rather hilarious, and stuck to his decision, which, as it happened, had been dictated by Strauss himself.

Frau Gutheil-Schoder's head cold thus turned out to be my great chance.

And yet in retrospect I am tempted to wonder if it was not fate rather than chance. Very often in my life I have had a feeling of being guided: portents of evil, seeming disasters tragic in their implications, frequently have turned out to be blessings in disguise. A greater power, far more knowledgeable than my own self in determining what is or is not good for me, has led me with a kindly hand. I feel this to be true.

My role as the Composer in *Ariadne auf Naxos* turned out to be decisive in determining my future success. Overnight I became "famous," and doors opened for me abroad.

I always have loved this role. Later on, when at Strauss's behest I sang Ariadne, I always used to stand backstage during the entire Prologue, listening to the Composer with longing in my heart and wishing that I could sing both roles at once.

The Prologue

Though Hofmannsthal based his libretto on Molière's *Le Bourgeois Gentilhomme*, he shifted the place of action from Paris to Vienna.

For the edification of his guests, the *nouveau riche* commissions an opera from a young, unknown composer, who for the occasion composes the tragic *Ariadne*. He thus offers what he believes to be a precious gift both to his patron's guests and to the world of music in general, vastly overestimating his client's musical sophistication. The latter, horrified at the very thought of having poor Ariadne live on the bleak island of Naxos rather than in luxurious surroundings more in keeping with the decor of his own home, decides to hire a troupe of entertainers for the express purpose of adding some spice and fun to this depressing opera. The troupe consists of the four standard characters of *opera buffa*, that is, Harlequin, Scaramuccio, Brighella, and Truffaldino, with the delightful *diseuse* Zerbinetta as special attraction. Their act is to come right after *Ariadne*. The Composer, upon learning that a cheap harlequinade is to dispel the impact of his tragic creation, rises in savage fury and rails at the insipid frivolity of mankind; he despises those smug, overstuffed Philistines, one and all. His honest hunger is worth more than all the exotic food they gorge on, his soul's longing more truly beautiful than all their silk and satin. Only a man starving, lonely, and misunderstood will have the courage to aim for the stars; but after this shattering experience, will he ever be able to improvise a tune again? This hideous world of platitudes has no room for melody. And yet . . . at this very moment, and in this of all places, a lovely tune comes to him out of nowhere, amid all the noise punctuated by the servants' humiliating and brash chatter, a tune hauntingly sweet and simple—his heart's own song. And he immediately hums it to his teacher, who listens with delight, sure that his stubborn, quick-tempered young charge will go on to brave insult and disappointment, hunger and privation, to storm the heavens if need be: his road is laid out in advance.

The brief glory of that moment is shattered by Zerbinetta, an earthy creature rooted in everyday reality and bent on sweeping aside anyone or anything that will not come to terms with it. The Composer takes another look at the comedians, and Zerbinetta, who had aroused his interest a few minutes earlier now stands revealed to him in all her petty vulgarity, a cheap little clown with whom he has nothing in common. He tears up the notes for his new song and slinks off, pouting in impotent rage.

Hofmannsthal put much humor into caricaturing the vulgarity of his stage singers. The vainglorious, insipid Prima Donna is made to prattle on endlessly about her "friends in high places," and the egomaniac Tenor always insists on having the most important role, which makes it rather hard for him to understand that Bacchus in the play is supposed to be a divine boy, a Greek god rather than a fat, conceited tenor swaddled in a leopard skin.

Emerging from their dressing rooms, they are outraged to hear that they will have to share the stage with a troupe of clowns. The Music Master, however, knows how to handle his charges; a bit of flattery quickly persuades the Prima Donna to change her mind. After all, how could a few dimwitted wandering minstrels possibly detract from her glory, and how could a stupid tenor hope to rival her success?

On the other side of the stage, meanwhile, the cunning Dancing Master is trying to calm down the infuriated Zerbinetta, who is afraid that *Ariadne* will bore the audience to tears before the players get a chance to prove their mettle. "Bored they will be, bored indeed," the Dancing Master agrees. "But that will make the contrast all the more striking. They'll wake up the moment you come onstage, and our Zerbinetta will be the Queen of the Evening and make them forget all about tedious prima donnas. . . ."

The mood now settles into one of general satisfaction. The Composer, too, has made peace with his fate, and the Music Master summons everyone to his place. But like a bombshell exploding in their midst comes the announcement by the Majordomo, who is transmitting an order from the Lord of the Manor: the two plays are to be presented simultaneously so as to provide for a change of pace. He obviously has read the libretto of *Ariadne* and has been horrified at the prospect of boring his guests or having them listen to Ariadne's continual complaints. Now he has decided to fix matters by a simple device: let them give the two plays at the same time.

For an instant the actors stand there, thunderstruck. But the comedians, adaptable, are quick to agree; they are used to strange requests, to patrons' whims, to sudden shifts and improvisations. The Dancing Master, in fact, regards the solution as eminently reasonable all around; a bleak desert island really strikes him as a poor background for a play. The Composer, on the other hand, is foaming at the mouth: they are deliberately ruining his creative work, wrecking its beauty, tearing it to bits; the entire opera will simply make no sense at all if Ariadne's lonely sorrow is to be troubled by vulgar humans. He wants to have nothing more to do with these crude Philistines, and is ready to storm out into the night, leave this mean-spirited abode in which they humiliate him and destroy his work. But the Music Master gently reminds him of the facts of life; one needs money in order to eat, and the evening's fee will give the Composer a whole year's freedom and security in which to create new and greater beauty. The Composer protests; he sees no chance for any real life at all in a world bent on killing the soul and letting the best of its children starve in body and spirit.

The Dancing Master, a member of the Players' Group, eavesdrops on this conversation in utter bewilderment. How can grown men be so unreasonable? Everything will work out well; his troupe is apt at improvisation. Zerbinetta, in fact, is a veritable genius in that difficult field. Any opera stands to gain from a few well-chosen additions that make the work more accessible to an average audience, and the Composer had better learn to accept this basic fact and come down out of the clouds if he wants a chance to hear his opera in actual performance.

With a passionate gesture, the Composer clutches the score to his bosom; rather consign it to the flames than thus prostitute his genius and his art.

But the Dancing Master talks him out of it by a series of glib arguments that eventually succeed in breaching the Composer's stubborn intransigence. After all, did not the greatest of masters have to make compromises and sacrifices infinitely more painful than this trifling and ridiculous comedy of errors? Still reluctant, the Composer gradually begins to accept the wily Dancing Master's arguments and starts to make drastic cuts and revisions under his guidance. In the meantime, the Tenor and the Prima Donna stand by, endeavoring to salvage their own parts, and trying to persuade the Composer in stage whispers to mutilate and cut the rival's role.

Zerbinetta now summarizes the plot of the opera for the benefit of her colleagues, and in the process reduces this passionate and moving tragedy to an insipid comedy, with the Composer vainly and wildly interrupting time and again, trying to convey the tragic significance of Ariadne and the por-

[9]

tent of the vast sea of loneliness all about her, a loneliness from which death alone can redeem her. As Ariadne beholds Bacchus, she mistakes him for Death—and it is to Death that she gives herself, though what she clings to in a passionate embrace turns out to be the essence of life itself, Bacchus leading her back into profound happiness.

At this, Zerbinetta explodes with laughter. Death? God, how funny! And as for Bacchus, he is a "gentleman friend of Ariadne's," as Zerbinetta puts it, a new suitor come to rescue her from intolerable boredom.

The Composer does not even bother listening to Zerbinetta's vulgar frivolities; in his mind's eye he beholds the vision of loneliness, the lovely face of Ariadne longing desperately for Death to release her. Zerbinetta, on the other hand, is not accustomed to being ignored or, for that matter, regarded as an unwelcome intrusion. Flirtatiously pursuing the Composer, she asks if her taking part in the opera will make it bad, and why. With a cry of despair the Composer flings himself into an armchair. At a sign from Zerbinetta, all the others leave the room. She has a way with men. True, she has never yet met up with so young, so wholesome and wholly uncorrupted a boy, but she will figure out a way of bringing him around to her point of view. Good heavens, a fat purse is involved, and this pigheaded fool with his highfalutin notions is likely to make them lose a lot of money. Nothing, absolutely nothing in the world is more important to Zerbinetta than money.

Playfully striking the Composer with her fan, Zerbinetta begins by cajoling. "After all," she pleads, "you have all your life ahead of you. There'll be many hours quite different from this one." The touch of Zerbinetta's fan, this slight, subtle gesture, has an electrifying effect upon the young man, who starts up abruptly, in utter confusion. What is it she is trying to tell him? Could there ever be another hour, even if he lived to be a hundred, more devastating and destructive than the one he is living through now? With all the disingenuous trust of innocence and youth, he listens to the cunning Zerbinetta as she acts out the role of a sadly misunderstood girl whose apparent frivolity is in truth a mask to shield her sensitive and vulnerable self, whose soul is a twin to his. Lonely, unloved, misunderstood, she is fated to travel alone.

The Composer is smitten. He can feel the kinship between them, and their vulgar surroundings sink into oblivion as their souls join in song.

His hand reaches out for hers with longing and passion, but Zerbinetta has no intention of getting involved with this silly youngster. Disengaging herself, holding him off, she improvises sweet nothings. Never, never will he forget this moment of bliss.

Zerbinetta leaves him in a state of heavenly turmoil.

At this point the Music Master returns to face open battle with the Prima Donna, who refuses outright to share the stage with Zerbinetta, a vulgar, cheap clown. He subdues her and then apprehensively turns to his student.

But the Composer is a man utterly transfigured, walking on clouds. The world is beautiful. Harmony reigns supreme. Courage is the source of power, courage rising out of music. Music is the Mother of the Arts, sending angels of courage to her children in distress.

The players' shrill shrieks and whistles drown the rest of this ecstatic hymn as they come tumbling onto the stage with screams and raucous laughter, leaping about like savages. Zerbinetta is right there with them. Zerbinetta belongs to their world.

The Composer rouses himself from his dream. How, even for the fraction of a second, could he ever have thought that all was well with the world? His teacher should never have let him consent to this cruel mutilation of a beautiful work of art. No, he wants nothing to do with it. He would rather starve, freeze to death, turn to cold stone if that is to be his fate. And off he strides, out into a barren loneliness vaster, more bleak than that surrounding Ariadne, one from which no Bacchus will come to rescue him. But his life will be in his art.

Ariadne auf Naxos
— the Opera

*T*HE CURTAIN RISES on a stage within a stage. The desert
island is provided with an impressive frame of gilded decora-
tions whose baroque ostentation surrounds the vision of bleak-
ness with the decor of conspicuous wealth. Yet the island
does stand out, its majesty aloof and undisturbed. Ariadne is
lying on the ground outside the grotto that affords her shelter,
alone except for the spirit companions, the elemental spirits
of nature who share her fate. They are Dryade, Naiade, and
Echo. Dryads inhabit trees as the soul inhabits the body;
naiads live in rivers or deep ponds. Echo is an ethereal creature,
an empty voice whose soulless song is like the rustle of the
wind; once upon a time she had been a beautiful nymph who
loved talk and laughter, a happy child whom Zeus began to
woo and whom jealous Hera punished by taking from her the
power of speech. Ever since then she has been mere empty
sound, able only to repeat the words of others, never uttering
one of her own. She fell in love with Narcissus, but, being unable to convey her feelings, could only gaze at him from afar;
and thus in unfulfilled longing she gradually wilted away,

[13]

with only her voice lingering on in the air, an empty voice echoing the words of others.

These, then, were Ariadne's companions.

The charming trio with which the opera opens contains the voices of Nature. Water flows in swiftly running tunes, branches seem to be moving in the wind, and the wind's own voice is added to theirs. The three nymphs are witnesses to Ariadne's wild grief, looking on without comprehension, for Nature is indifferent to human suffering and can only offer a gentle lullaby. Ariadne stirs and wakens with a plaintive outcry: a dream tormented her sleep, a dream now forgotten like a fugitive shadow. But her heart is doomed to suffering, and her whole being is torn by yearning for him, the unfaithful one.

Pliant and gentle, Echo repeats her plaintive "Oh."

At this point the players of the traveling show feel that an interruption is called for, something to perk up the proceedings; you cannot expect an audience to sit still all night while this woman carries on about her long-lost lover.

Therefore they creep up on Ariadne, meanwhile deliberating among themselves as to how best to comfort her. She pays no attention to them, immersed in her dreams of the past, her unforgettable happiness by the side of Theseus. At the same time she begins to suspect that giving herself over so completely to her grief and longing may be slightly humiliating. There must be a road to oblivion. If she could but forget the name—Theseus. But how could she ever forget what is part of her very soul?

The three nymphs call out her name, imploring and beseeching. All is quiet around her, peaceful, except for her grief drowning out the gentle sounds of Nature.

Ariadne refuses to listen to the nymphs and plunges back into her private sorrow, wallowing in memories of her previous existence, which had been pure, wholesome, unburdened by worries. There must be release for her somewhere, and the only release she craves is death. The end. Final deliverance.

The players are utterly mystified and decide that Ariadne must be insane. Therefore they proceed to administer the only medicine they are familiar with.

They give her music, with Harlequin pouring his very soul into his performance until Zerbinetta, accustomed to being the center of men's attention, feigns jealousy and makes a scene. This is the sort of thing the audience is likely to appreciate and applaud, something saucy and real rather than exalted sighs from the depths of a noble heart.

Once again Ariadne rises above her vulgar surroundings and, in an ecstatic transfiguration, summons Death to take her as a lover, forever and ever. She stands like a statue, with arms raised in a passionate appeal.

This really upsets the players, who now decide to go all out to bring some life to this place. Apparently intent on cheering up Ariadne, they begin to encircle her in a playful dance. But she remains motionless and unmoved, paying no heed. Zerbinetta, realizing that their efforts are vain, sends away her colleagues and, alone with Ariadne, begins to expound at some length her philosophy of life, which is rather at loggerheads with that of the noble Ariadne. Why, of course Zerbinetta realizes that having your lover run out on you is no fun, that for him to leave you stuck on a bleak, dull island like this is downright mean. But good heavens, the world is full of nice, interesting men. You have a choice—and you choose. It is as simple as that, and merely more of the same every time, no matter how often you fool yourself into thinking that this is going to be "it," that this is different. Heart pounding, you go out to meet your fate, a godlike creature—until you get to know him a little better; then you start looking around for somebody else. She, Zerbinetta, ought to know all about it. As a matter of fact, sometimes she has been in love with two men at the same time, passionately devoted to both of them.

Ariadne, however, already has disappeared into her grotto, withdrawn from a world with which she has nothing in common.

Harlequin enters, pleasantly surprised to find Zerbinetta all alone. He begins to court her with plain words and gestures. Soon he is joined by his three fellow players. Zerbinetta enjoys herself hugely. Four men to choose from, four men dancing attendance upon her . . .

At last she makes up her mind and chooses Harlequin—for the time being. She runs off with him, leaving the others behind in confusion and disappointment.

The crazy comedy thus has come to an end. Now the singers of the regular opera reappear on the stage. The three nymphs sweep across the stage, excited, for all Nature is in turmoil: a great god is about to arrive aboard a mighty ship, a god who may deliver Ariadne from her grief. The nymphs have learned the story of how he escaped the wiles of Circe; wind, water, and the rustle of the trees have spread news of the event, the god's great triumph. And now he is about to arrive.

They summon Ariadne to witness the arrival.

The voice of Bacchus rises in the distance, singing of Circe and wondering what it was that she wanted to do to him and why. What happens to those who fail to resist her?

Slowly Ariadne, as though drawn by that marvelous voice, emerges from the grotto. She is convinced that it is Death himself, the redeemer, come to take her away; and with her eyes closed she waits for him in a pose of trembling expectation.

The nymphs in the meantime are singing a sweet, simple tune to welcome him, a tune reminiscent of the Schubert lullaby *"Schlafe, schlafe, holder süsser Knabe . . ."*

(I remember a piano rehearsal which Strauss suddenly interrupted. "I must have stolen this from Schubert," he burst out in startled amusement, actually blushing with embarrassment.)

Bacchus keeps on singing about the quaintly bittersweet confusion into which he was plunged by his adventure. Although he did escape, Circe's magic potion seems to go on working in his blood and beclouding his senses.

Ariadne, on the other hand, breaks out in rousing music. Death's own messenger has come at last. Death has sent for her, Death for whom she has been craving since she lost Theseus. She is ready, more than ready.

And while Bacchus goes on singing, she lifts up her hands and, turning, gathers all her courage to gaze upon his countenance. His beauty is almost more than she can bear; standing there in an aureole of light and glory, he looks like Theseus returned. In spite of herself, she cries out the name of her unfaithful lover.

But she checks herself at once. This is not Theseus, the unforgotten and unforgettable one. This is Death, she knows, Death come to deliver her from this vale of tears. And with a deep bow she greets in him "the messenger of messengers."

I must digress here with a rather funny experience. Lack of concentration not being one of my habitual sins, I still do not know how it happened that one night I completely forgot the long welcoming speech. Worse, though, was my inexplicable conviction, that the phrase "Welcome, O messenger of messengers" was to be sung by Bacchus rather than by myself, so that, when I heard the prompter's desperate whisper, I kept wondering why on earth the tenor refused to sing his phrase. All through that performance I failed to realize my inexcusable error. Afterwards, however, Strauss, with a laugh, asked me about it. "Were you that unhappy about not getting Theseus back? Bacchus, it seems to me, is a highly eligible and attractive substitute." At that point the full extent of my crime suddenly became clear to me, and I asked his forgiveness, which he granted in the most charming manner by sending me a postcard photograph of himself, autographed and with the obverse side reading:

Because  was so beautiful, Lottchen's punishment will be lightened to the extent that at the next *Ariadne* performance the phrase

will need to be sung *only twice*. In spite of which it really was *very beautiful!* In gratitude, your most faithful admirer.
Vienna, April 12, 1931.

As a conductor, Strauss was the most magnanimous person with whom I ever have worked. He never showed agitation over mistakes made by the individual performer, but always concentrated on the total effect.

In this connection, another anecdote characteristic of the man: A famous colleague of mine, who, like myself, tended toward a certain laxness in the fine points of musical precision, was singing at a rehearsal conducted by Franz Schalk. It happened to be a Strauss opera, and the composer himself, standing next to the conductor, was outraged at the obvious liberties taken by the singer, whom otherwise he greatly respected. It seemed to him that the part was being completely distorted. Seething with anger, he strode to the back of the theater, voicing his protest. Then, from the back he went on listening, and gradually his fury gave way to a smile. He walked up to the front again, and in a whisper informed the conductor that all was well. "No harm done. She sings so divinely that it really doesn't matter."

Thus that he accepted my apologies with such easy grace came as no great surprise.

But let us return to Ariadne.

Bacchus calmly turns to Ariadne, believing her to be the goddess of the island. He has learned to approach goddesses with diffidence. After all, she may turn out to be another Circe, bent on transmuting him into some beast or other and robbing him of his innocence.

Ariadne, however, fails to understand. She is numb with confusion. And now that her desire for death is about to be fulfilled, she senses a quavering weakness within herself. How long has she been waiting for this blessed moment? How long is it since Theseus deserted her?

Bacchus, who heard her call him Theseus when first she laid eyes on him, is curious, but Ariadne refuses to explain. No, she knows that he has come to take her away on his ship, take her to where she will find eternal rest, and so be it.

Bacchus is profoundly aroused. He realizes that this strange, beautiful creature is longing for death; but he, the God of Joy, is not going to let her die. Both fire and balm flow in his veins; his mother died by fire when his father Zeus, giving way to her blasphemous wish, revealed himself to her in his divine image, and that same consuming fire now flows in his veins along with the exuberant joy of living. He would sooner do to death the stars eternal under heaven's vault than harm Ariadne.

Ariadne is overwhelmed, unable still to realize that this is not Death come to fetch her. She feels the magic spell of the god's words, and the world about her vanishes.

Fainting, she sinks into Bacchus's arms and gone is the dreary grotto, and in its stead a brilliant, star-studded sky covers them like a canopy. Frightened, trembling like a lost child, she holds him off, gazing up in wonder at the great transformation. As his kiss brushes her forehead, she thinks that the hour of death has come, and shyly asks if they are already in the Great Beyond, in the blessed realm of Death.

Bacchus, profoundly moved, takes her into his arms, and, impelled by their ecstatic affirmation of life, they both rise into the clouds as a golden canopy descends upon them.

The nymphs sing their lullaby, and Zerbinetta, who has to put in her two cents' worth, points out that the story ends just as she had predicted.

The opera concludes with a beautiful duet as Ariadne, now knowingly restored to happiness and life, lies in the arms of Bacchus, and the canopy becomes their bridal chamber.

Legend has it that Bacchus gave Ariadne a resplendent crown as a wedding present and that after her death—for she was mortal, after all—he flung it up into the skies, whence it still casts its light upon the earth. I often have gazed up at the skies and been moved at the sight of this crown, which made the whole story come to life for me.

Our Ariadne performance was the masterpiece of both the director, Wymetal, and the stage designer Alfred Roller, not to mention Franz Schalk's authoritative musical direction. Bacchus was sung by the Hungarian singer Béla von Környey, endowed with a splendid voice but rather remote from the ideal of a Greek god in outward appearance. Later on, the part was taken over by the great singing actor Karl Aagard-Oestvig, and now it was a young god indeed who made his entrance on the stage. I shall never forget the sight of him as he appeared high on the rock, a luminous red coat half covering him, a leopard skin slung around his hips, and a gold ribbon in his hair, which had been dyed black for the occasion (by nature he was a blond Viking). The ecstatic outcry "Theseus" always sounded most convincing when he was the object. Aagard-Oestvig rose like a dazzling meteor in the star-studded skies of the opera world, but, alas, like a meteor he burned out all too soon. As far as I know, he is now living in his native Norway with his beautiful wife, once a charming soprano at the Vienna Opera. I never was able to understand why he left the stage when he did, at the very height of his career, regarded as one of the most valuable assets of our company. Later on, whenever a new production or a new cast was discussed, someone invariably would bring up Aagard-Oestvig as the "ideal man for the part." The meteor was not to be forgotten.

Ariadne was sung by Maria Jeritza, moving in her beauty, noble in every motion, and rousing in her song. Her blonde hair was hidden under a red wig, and a cornflower-colored garment draped her slender shape in flowing folds.

Hans Duhan, a charming singer and actor, had the dual role of the Music Master and Harlequin.

Zerbinetta was sung by the unforgettable Selma Kurz, not an outstanding actress, but so wholly accomplished in the art of singing, with a voice so irresistibly warm and sweet, that actually she did a perfect job.

The Dancing Master was Georg Maikl, that good and ever reliable tenor with his resonant, indestructible voice.

The opera calls for a chamber orchestra, a fact utilized by Alfred Roller, the great stage designer, to enlarge the already huge stage by covering part of the orchestra pit, which proved a very effective innovation.

An elite audience attended the premiere, and the only time I ever again saw anything remotely like it in splendor and elegance was the reopening of the Vienna State Opera in 1955. Those were still the good old times, when everyone present dressed with the careful, formal, resplendent elegance that was and should be part of the opera. An opera performance ought to be a formal, festive occasion, and attendance should be planned and prepared for in advance rather than incidentally or on the spur of the moment. I still feel this way, though I realize that times have changed. Well, just as long as the audience does not start munching sandwiches and opening cans of tuna fish during the performance, as I saw one do during the revolution. Those days, too, are gone, thank God. And there is something precious about memories of splendor and glory past, no matter how incomprehensible or even ridiculous they may seem to the present generation. When I let myself go and think of the Vienna Opera in the days long ago, I tend to lose myself until I have trouble finding my way back to the present.

Die Frau ohne Schatten

I HAD DECIDED to devote the entire year of 1919 to much-needed rest and leisure. After my success as the Composer in *Ariadne auf Naxos*, I had sung all too often in many different roles until I had found myself utterly exhausted, craving nothing but complete relaxation. With my parents I went to the village of Gmunden on the beautiful Traunsee in Upper Austria, determined to use my vacation not only to recover from physical and mental stress, but also to go on a diet—made necessary, alas, because I was weak-willed indeed when faced with Viennese pastry. In the large gymnasium of the Gmunden Sanatorium, I took wild rides on an electrically operated horse, rowed a stationary boat that went nowhere, and had massage belts shake me up from head to toe, melting away all superfluous fat and improving my shape.

Once in a while, however, I would trade the electric boat for a real one, and glide slowly across the silvery blue of the lake. Now and then I met a motorboat with a—to me—fascinating passenger, the daughter of the Emperor Wilhelm II, who had found a refuge and a home at the castle of her father-in-law, the Duke of Cumberland. The monarchy had fallen by then, we were living under a republican form of government, and by rights I no longer should have let myself be impressed by the sight of royalty. My heart, however, beat faster whenever I met this rather kindly looking lady, to whom, I, as a child, always had referred as "the Little Princess." We would spend hours in Berlin waiting to catch a glimpse of her as she passed in her carriage, rewarding us with a friendly smile and a wave of her hand. The world, which had taken so much from her, had not been able to rob her of her innate kindness, and she always smiled at me when our boats met on the lake.

I often had cause to regret not keeping a diary. Now, for instance, I have no way of checking whether or not I gave a concert at Gmunden that summer. I rather believe I did sing at an affair organized on behalf of some local charities, for I seem to remember the Duke of Cumberland and his family attending. At any rate, this ultimately led to a dinner invitation at the castle. I was, of course, rather excited and awed by the feudal splendor, but I also had a marvelous time, especially with the old Duke, whom I reduced to a state of near collapse from laughter by describing to him the details of my reducing cure, especially my "electric" horsemanship.

The following day I received a charming brooch from "the Little Princess" as a memento of the occasion. Revolution or no revolution, I was delighted.

It seemed as though this would be the only break in the otherwise pleasantly dull routine, but something much more exciting was to follow.

One day a large package arrived unannounced. It turned out to be the piano score of Richard Strauss's new opera, *Die Frau ohne Schatten* (The Woman Without a Shadow), along with a letter from my beloved manager, Schalk, in which he implored me not to send it back by return mail, as was my custom (all my life I have suffered from an inferiority complex). That procedure would merely be a waste of time: I *had* to sing the role of the Dyer's Wife, if for no other reason than that it had been written especially for me. There was absolutely no point in my playing hard to get and making him get down on his knees before I gave in and accepted. In other words, he concluded, make believe that this score was sent to you once before.

Die Frau ohne Schatten contains two important female roles, the Empress and the Dyer's Wife. I have no idea when Strauss and Schalk chose me for the Dyer's Wife, but in a magazine article some time ago Maria Jeritza stated that Strauss originally wanted her to be the Dyer's Wife, but that he changed his mind and gave her the role of the Empress. If she said so, it must be true. Even so, I do not believe that I was merely second choice. I am convinced that I had been picked for one of the two roles, neither of which would have been a disappointment.

During the Second World War all my property in Vienna was lost; along with it, many precious letters from Strauss and Schalk went up in flames, among them correspondence begging me not to turn down this truly forbidding and vocally exhausting role.

They did not need to try very hard; I was much too ambitious, much too taken with the beauty of the music and fascinated by the psychologically fascinating personality of the Dyer's Wife to have entertained a thought of refusal.

The premiere was scheduled for October, which meant farewell to vacation, rest, and relaxation. I had to begin at once to study my part, and that raised the problem of finding an accompanist. One scarcely would have dared to hope that in a place like Gmunden someone able to cope with a score of extraordinary complexity would turn up. But miracles happen everywhere, even at Gmunden.

Two young men, also vacationers, had aroused my curiosity. One was Jascha Hornstein, who became a well-known conductor, but at that time was a rather wild-and-woolly-looking Bohemian; the other was Leo Sirota, who became a well-known pianist. I asked the latter to help me, and he more than rose to the occasion.

Strauss, in the meantime, sent me an invitation to spend the rest of the summer as his guest at Garmisch. He had a lovely home there in the mountains, and I could combine a pleasant vacation with the arduous task of learning my role. I accepted with pleasure, timing my arrival so that I would already have a fair conception of my part in its broad musical aspects.

For me to have faced Strauss wholly unprepared would have been utterly inconceivable; I always have made a practice of studying a role first in the privacy of my own home, of laying the ground work there. Though I happen to be a rather poor pianist, my competence always has proved sufficient to help me in mastering the initial difficulties.

Time and again I now see young singers appear at the initial piano rehearsals utterly innocent of any advance knowledge, completely unprepared, having to be literally dragged from one note to the next by pitiable instructors endowed with the patience of angels.

Strauss was greatly amazed at my knowing even a single phrase of the work, and time and again expressed both his surprise and delight. "God," he would cry out, "that's really a tough one! I'd never have thought that any singer could learn this."

The house itself was beautiful. Dr. Franz Strauss, the composer's son, still lives there with his family.

I happened to meet Dr. Strauss a few years ago at a Munich Festival performance of *Arabella*, and he later wrote to tell me how well he still remembered that summer when I was their guest at Garmisch, so hard at work with his father, so wholly dedicated, and so utterly devoid of any desire for the now all-important "publicity."

This was my first opportunity for personal contact with Strauss. As a rule he appeared utterly aloof and impersonal, so cold in his reaction to people that they would withdraw instantly and give up any misguided attempt at chumminess. But there in his home I came to know an altogether different Strauss. Or rather, I saw in him two different personalities. The morning hours were given over to work, and work in a sense in which I had never known it before. No hour was too long, no amount of sunshine could lure him away from the piano, and I felt that in all my life filled with hard work I never had really known before what it meant for a musician to be working.

He made few suggestions regarding my interpretation of the role; I believe that, for one thing, he liked my own approach and that, for another, he disliked making changes. This was also the case later on during the full rehearsals. But the phrasing and the divinely inspired music were developed and worked out. At times he seemed to be sitting there with tears in his eyes, but I kept thinking that perhaps my imagination was playing tricks on me; the chill and impersonal Strauss could not possibly, now, could he? . . .

Who ever can describe another human being truly or even presume to understand him? How much less, then, can one hope to understand the genius of a man endowed by God? It has been said of Strauss that he was a first-rate businessman interested mainly in getting his operas on the boards so that he could collect royalties. The statement is ridiculous; one might as well say that a father loves his children only because they may someday support him in his old age.

To Strauss, his operas and his music were his life, the children of his genius; he loved them and in turn wanted to see them famous, beloved by the whole world. That he also possessed a measure of sound business sense in no way detracts from the creative achievements of his genius.

His character was full of contradictions, a phenomenon natural enough—only a dull and colorless person can be wholly consistent. As it happened, I came to know yet another aspect of Strauss during those days: the henpecked and rather subdued husband. His wife, Pauline, nimble-witted and with a caustic tongue, derived an almost perverse pleasure from proving to her husband that no amount of fame could alter her personal opinion of him as essentially nothing but a peasant, a country yokel.

Strauss himself warded her off with an indulgent smile, not even bothering to listen while she explained in great detail how and why their marriage constituted, in fact, a shocking *mésalliance* as far as she was concerned; she could have married a dashing young hussar. Nor was his music, as she readily explained to all who would listen, anywhere near comparable to that of Massenet. She in fact behaved like a shrew, snapping and snarling at him whenever and wherever she could, but I suspect that actually he rather enjoyed it all. "Believe me, Lotte," he said to me the day I was leaving, "the whole world's admiration interests me a great deal less than a single one of Pauline's fits of rage."

He loved her truly and profoundly, and the words he wrote for his opera *Intermezzo* came from the depths of his own faithful heart: "This is what I call a truly happy marriage."

Pauline Strauss merits a chapter all to herself.

Born into an ancient and aristocratic family of officers, she affected contempt for the world of art, though as a former opera singer she had been part of it at least briefly. All her passion, energy, and ambition were concentrated on being a housewife, and she raised cleanliness to a private cult practiced with ruthless fanaticism. Any visitor to her home, no matter what his rank, age, or station in life, was welcomed by her peremptory: "Wipe your feet."

The house was a model of order and antiseptic cleanliness, and one literally could have eaten off the floor—except that Pauline would never have permitted it. Her closets were arranged like showcases, each object wrapped in silk cloth and the contents set up in rows or stacked in piles as straight as though they had been laid out with ruler and plumb line; whenever I looked at them, I felt like a gypsy roaming the world in a wagon, sloppy and neglectful.

(Later on she once paid me a visit in Vienna. Unfortunately I happened to be out at the time, and on my return the maid resentfully reported how Pauline had opened all our closets and ordered change made, thenceforth and at once. "Nothing I could do about it, Madame," the maid kept wailing. "She paid no attention to me, just went right on from one closet to the next." Knowing Pauline, I could imagine her utterly horrified indignation at the sight that had met her stern eyes, and I laughed till I was in tears.)

The masseuse came every morning, and her arrival was the signal for Strauss to go for a walk. He simply could not bear listening to the tortured screams of his beloved wife; for the masseuse happened to be of the school that believes in the kind of massage during which the flesh is torn off the bones, and Pauline trusted her implicitly, honestly convinced that at last she had found the one person who could help improve her health. Neither her health nor her figure actually needed improvement, as far as I could tell; though not very tall, she was slender, youthful in appearance, well built, and attractive. Why in the world she insisted on undergoing those daily torture sessions was something I never understood.

More understandable was the fact that she found me rather on the heavy side; there was, I admit, some justification for this opinion on her part. But when she recommended her masseuse while gleefully squeezing my arm and exclaiming over the amount of excess flesh that would have to come off, I fled in horror after expressing my thanks.

I did, however, do setting-up exercises with Pauline every morning, and I am sure they did me no harm. But I remember how one morning, when the two of us were lying half-naked on the floor of the terrace (fresh air being absolutely essential to this sort of thing), Strauss by mistake opened the door, shut it again, and ran off in deadly embarrassment, paying no heed to Pauline's shouted orders to come back and join us instead of running away. I was afraid that, dutiful husband that he was, he would obey; but for once he had the courage of his cowardice.

In the evening he would often accompany me in his Lieder. The whole marvelous world of the Lied was unknown and uncharted territory to me at that period in my life, though my voice was probably good enough to cover up my lack of familiarity with the charm of fresh naïveté. At any rate, I enjoyed those occasions very much: Pauline always would be in an exceptionally gentle mood, listening to the songs that perhaps reminded her of the early days of their courtship. I often caught a glance or a smile passing between her and her husband, touching in its love and happiness, and I began to sense something of the profound affection between those two human beings, a tie so elemental in strength that none of Pauline's shrewish truculence ever could trouble it seriously.

In fact, I rather suspect that they were always putting on a kind of act for their own benefit as well as for that of outsiders, and that in her heart of hearts Pauline knew perfectly well how much her "Richardl," as she used to call him in tender moments, understood and loved her just the way she was.

In her younger days she had sung many a concert with

Richard accompanying her on the piano, and her store of anecdotes on the subject was priceless. She always would make her entrance wearing a scarf that she could unwind and toss away with a dramatic flourish, thus drawing the attention of the audience to herself exclusively—a story she told with a truly devilish gleam in her eyes. And whenever one of those hateful, endless codas of his would force her to stand quietly and give way to *his* music, she would contrive to take a deep bow, thus forcing the audience to applaud and interrupt the music, which must have caused raised eyebrows all around. But in any case she would once again have carried the day.

Strauss, who in all likelihood had heard each one of these stories time and again, would smile indulgently and gaze at his capricious wife in both wonder and tender delight. I sometimes expected him to lose his temper, but he never did. The only possible explanation is that he saw and valued her as she really was—a jewel in a very rough setting.

But there was one corner in that antiseptic model home that even Pauline in her fanatical cleanliness did not dare to touch—Strauss's desk. At least I firmly want to believe this to be so. That was where he wrote *Die Frau ohne Schatten*, and where I had the rare good fortune to study my part with him personally. It was a part incredibly difficult and demanding, but supreme as an artistic challenge.

Die Frau ohne Schatten is not popular in the United States, where I am now living, and I do not believe that it will ever become a popular favorite despite the overpowering beauty of its music. The libretto is intricate, ornate, overloaded, and very hard to follow; several very good synopses outline the plot of the opera, so that here I shall concentrate on giving a deeper insight into the characters, just as I tried to do with *Ariadne*.

The fundamental idea serving as basis to the plot is that a marriage not blessed by children cannot offer perfect happiness. This problem confronts two couples in the opera, the first a supernatural Empress married to a human Emperor, the other a Dyer and his Wife.

For some reason the Dyer is the only character in the entire opera to whom Hofmannsthal gave a name. He is Barak the Dyer, whereas neither his Wife nor the Imperial Couple have proper names. Nameless also is the "Nurse," a demonic hag of great importance to the story.

Act One

The curtain rises upon a dark stage illumined only by a soft glow from the chambers of the Imperial Couple. Outside on the palace steps, doglike, lies the Nurse, keeping watch over her beautiful mistress, who now shares the Emperor's bed though once upon a time she had been the daughter of Keikobad, Lord of the Spirit World, and able to assume whatever shape she desired. But once, when in the guise of a white gazelle she roamed in joyful freedom through the moss-covered forests, she encountered the Emperor, who happened to be out hunting and who immediately pursued this rare and beautiful prey. The white gazelle proved much the faster and would have escaped had it not been for the trained falcon poised on the Emperor's arm. Flapping its wings, the bird blinded the gazelle, forcing it to halt—and just as the Emperor was about to close in for the kill, the gazelle changed back into her own true self, daughter of Keikobad, a creature of miraculous beauty. In the Emperor's arms she thus not only became her own self again, but also learned something she had never known before, the supreme joy of love. In due course she married the Emperor and went to live with him at his palace, taking along her faithful Nurse, who, though utterly devoted and ready to follow her charge anywhere, also was deeply resentful at seeing her "untouchable" darling lower herself to become the Emperor's willing victim. The Nurse hates the Emperor and patiently bides her time, waiting for Keikobad's vengeance, which she knows is about to strike.

A fiery glow in the distance makes her look up; could it be Keikobad, come to reclaim his daughter at last, after eleven long moons? It turns out to be Keikobad's messenger, announcing that the Empress has three more days to live with her husband; if at the end of those three days she still fails to cast a shadow—in other words, if she has not yet become truly human, but continues to belong to the spirit world ruled over by her father—she must return to him. As to the Emperor, in punishment for his audacity in trying to drag a child of the spirit world down to him into the sphere of humans, he shall turn to stone.

"Turn to stone . . . In this, indeed, I see the hand of Keikobad, and I bow to his messenger," the Nurse says in somber triumph. She well knows that Keikobad's cruel judgment will cause her mistress suffering and grief, but they will be going home at last, and the splendor of the spirit world will soon efface the memory of the Emperor. Or so, at least, the Nurse reasons.

The messenger vanishes just as the Emperor appears in the doorway. He is young and beautiful, but the Nurse, though paying her respects to him in the surliest manner possible, sees in him only her mistress's seducer.

He announces that he will be gone for three days, not suspecting that those three days will turn out to be the most important of his life. He is off to hunt eagles in the vast forests of his realm. But before leaving, he sings of his love for the Empress and orders the Nurse to tell her that he lives but for her.

The music of this aria is of singular beauty, and I still to this day remember Aagard-Oestvig singing the part of the Emperor at the premiere. He was particularly dazzling in this scene, overwhelming in a strangely and mysteriously magnetic way that held all of us captive.

The Emperor leaves without his beloved hunting falcon, for in the passionate intoxication of his first love, unable to bear the thought of any creature, even a falcon, having touched the eyes of his beloved, he had wounded the bird that always had served him so faithfully. In a sudden fit of anger he had speared the bird, which flew away, leaving a trail of blood, and never had returned.

The Emperor now rushes off, leaving the Nurse to spin her black thoughts about the three days ahead, three more days fraught with danger because a shadow may yet appear at the slender feet of her mistress.

Now the mistress is approaching, and the Nurse quickly sends away the other servants, for no one is allowed to behold the Empress face to face. The only human being she has ever come to know is her husband; no one else is admitted to her presence, and no mere human eyes shall feast upon the Pure One.

The Empress, emerging from her chambers, stretches sensuously; all her gestures are charged with the memory of the pleasure of the Emperor's embrace. Voices had awakened her prematurely—the Emperor and the Nurse conversing—though she would have liked to go on resting, dreaming of the one thing she now misses, the power to change her shape. How happy she would be could she but follow the beloved on his hunt, a white gazelle once again feeling the wings of the falcon above her and reliving that first clear look into the eyes of the man who taught her the meaning of love. Looking up into the sky she spies the falcon and suppresses a cry—the beloved bird has come back to them. But instead of swooping down, the falcon spreads its wings, and blood mixed with tears drips from them. "Woe unto me," the Empress hears the bird's plaintive voice. "Woe unto me. The woman casts no shadow, and the Emperor shall turn to stone. . . ."

The Empress now remembers the half-forgotten curse that went with the loss of her magic powers: "The woman shall cast no shadow. The Emperor shall turn to stone." She had forgotten it in the vast surge of happiness which had been hers, that she could not truly be a woman until, like mortal woman, she could cast a shadow. "The Emperor shall turn to stone. . . ." With a wild cry she turns to her Nurse, the wise, the all-knowing one: "Where, oh where shall I find a shadow?" But the Nurse, hard as though she were made of stone herself, merely remarks sneeringly that he who had the blasphemous temerity to touch the untouchable still seems to have proved incapable of completing his wife's transfiguration. Hatred colors her voice as she announces that the Emperor now will have to pay the price for those eleven moons of bliss.

The Empress realizes that Keikobad, her father, is bent on vengeance, that he will turn her beloved husband to stone, petrify the mouth that taught her how to kiss, the hand that caressed her. But she refuses to give up without a fight because deep down in her heart she feels herself to be stronger than her father. Love has given her self-knowledge, and with it knowledge of her own strength; she knows that she will find a shadow if she can only persuade the wise old Nurse to help her.

In vain the Nurse attempts to remind her charge in harsh tones that orders are made to be obeyed, that commands must be carried out. In the end she gives in, yielding to the will of the stronger one, the lover. Reluctantly she explains that they will have to descend to the world of ordinary humans, live with them, expose themselves to their pestilential breath. Peo-

ple are treacherous, stupid, cunning, and the Empress will
never learn to understand them, but she will have to risk it
just the same if she insists on finding a shadow.

The Empress, paying scant heed to the Nurse's contemptuous rantings, agrees to the plan. "A new day is breaking,"
she sings.

"A new day is breaking—the day of people, of human beings," the Nurse echoes with a sneer. What can the Empress
in her pristine purity possibly know about lust and greed?
But though the Nurse is fiercely opposed to the ultimate purpose of the plan, she does begin to enjoy the thought of its
actual execution because she derives pleasure from deceiving
people, lying to them, cheating the cheaters, stealing from
thieves.

"I'll catch on fast enough to their dirty tricks. I'll trap them
in their own snares; that's my one great talent."

Fear and horror suddenly grip the Empress, who until now
has never been brushed by evil and who now hears her beloved Nurse plotting and scheming base deeds. The Nurse, in
turn, perceiving the moment of weakness, is quick to exploit
it: "I see you trembling—are you afraid? Do you already rue
your desire? Shall we leave, forget about the shadow?"

But no fear or horror will stay the Empress's determination
to save her beloved, to find a shadow and thus to destroy the
curse. "Let us descend, then, down . . ."

To the strains of winged music the two of them descend
from the heights of splendor to the depths of human misery.
Discords streak the melody, and it is as though the two were
descending through leaden skies into the shrieking dissonance
of the everyday world. The flight takes them straight to the
shabby hut of an abysmally poor couple whose deep-rooted
conflicts the Nurse hopefully regards as offering exactly the
right soil for her devious plans.

They first observe the scene from a distance, themselves unseen, the Nurse greatly enjoying the sight before them. Nothing but fights and quarrels, spite and hatred wherever they look. The head of the household chosen by them is Barak the Dyer, a man who embodies everything that is good and true and noble in a human being, who nevertheless is hated by his own Wife with what appears to be all-consuming hatred. Actually, however, the woman suffers from ambivalent hate-love quite as much as he himself suffers from her bizarre and incomprehensible moods. They have been married for two and a half years, but as yet no child has blessed their home, and the woman, longing for fulfillment as wife and mother, vents her frustration and bitter disappointment upon her husband. She simply cannot bear his even-tempered, ever-loving, kindhearted goodness: it drives her insane, and furthermore she cannot see why his three Brothers, crippled and misshapen creatures whom she hates and despises, must share their hut. Barak, however, feels responsible for his Brothers, so cruelly dealt with by fate; he wants to be a father to them, make a home for them. It is for them as well as for his Wife that he goes out to work.

The Brothers, shiftless and lazy, with no responsibilities and nothing to occupy their hands, pass all their time fighting and brawling among themselves. The only bond among them is common hatred for their sister-in-law, that shrew who is trying to give them a hard time and wants nothing so much as to get rid of them altogether.

As the curtain rises, the three Brothers are once again battling among themselves. The Wife appears in the door, but instead of acting on her hatred and letting the men fight and perhaps even kill one another, she makes a futile attempt to separate them.

And this is very much part of her profoundly contradictory nature: though capable of passionate hatred, she does not want to destroy and is led to help even where by all logic she ought to look the other way. Here again she acts out of this contradiction and picks up the first thing handy, a pail full of water, which she dumps out on the brawlers to make them see reason. Her interference succeeds all too well, for now the three of them turn on her in strident fury, shouting insults and imprecations. Who does she think she is, anyway? Where does she get off, acting as if she owned the place? And why does she carry on as if she couldn't stand her husband when actually she likes to have him make love to her? She's a woman, just like any other—why can't their brother let her go? There are more where she came from.

Paralyzed, the Wife listens to their threats and curses, petrified with shame and horror at the thought that those three evidently were spying and eavesdropping on her and her husband as they made love at night. Night, those precious hours when she belonged to her husband without afterthoughts or reservations, cleansed of her hatred. She is a woman proud and pure of thought, hurt to the quick of her being; and as her husband arrives, she confronts him on the spot with an ultimatum: either they go or she goes: there is no room here for both them and her.

Barak, who has been exposed to this particular demand often enough, calmly scolds his Brothers and sends them off to take care of some small chores; they will be back in time for dinner. The Wife paces back and forth like a caged tigress, while Barak tackles his work of sorting the dyed skins to be taken to market. "Either they get out of here," she snarls, "and this time for good, or else I'm going. I want to find out how much I really mean to you."

How, she thinks, can he possibly hesitate to grant her this one wish? Isn't she worth more to him than those three good-for-nothing bums sponging off him, living from the fruits of his labor as though it were their God-given right? And why, if he truly loves her, does he shut his eyes to her sufferings and let those beasts torment her with their sneers and curses?

Barak, however, feels in honor bound to help and support his unfortunate Brothers. They, too, were innocent babies once upon a time, and in his father's house there was always food enough for thirteen children. Slowly he rises, halting just behind his Wife. "Give me children," he says quietly. "I promise you that they shall never go hungry." But as he touches her, a shudder as though of revulsion grips his Wife; passionate lover that she is at night, she turns into his enemy at the break of day. He desperately tries to understand her and now wants to believe the rumors current among his relatives and neighbors who say that she actually is pregnant but does not want to tell him about it, refuses to let him in on the one secret above all others that would make him happy, this being a result of the same strange contradictions in her character. This is his great hope, and he sees in it the solution to the mystery, having been told that the emotional state of a pregnant woman often is volatile and unpredictable. He accepts this as he does everything else, serenely, waiting for the happy day when she will give birth to their child.

His utterance of this hope is followed by a lengthy interlude of gently flowing, warm and moving music which with supreme artistry expresses Barak's emotions.

I had been giving some thought to the problem of what I could possibly do during that musical interlude. The last preceding phrase that I had sung consisted of a violent outburst against Barak, and right after the interlude I was to resume the same pitch of undiminished fury. Dramatically I felt somewhat at sea, and I asked Strauss what he thought I ought to do. "Do?" he asked in turn. "Nothing. Absolutely nothing at all. Why must you be doing something? After all, in real life people don't keep running back and forth all the time, do they? Just stand there quietly and *think yourself into the meaning of your role.* I'm sure you'll find the right sort of expression."

Strauss's simple explanation actually contained a valuable hint as to the nature of acting. One must have the courage to stand still, to "act" without "action," and one's thoughts must be so wholly concentrated and lucidly powerful as to be perceptibly convincing. To me, this was a revelation.

Later on Bruno Walter, the greatest teacher I had during my career on the stage, confirmed this concept. I still remember clearly how he helped me get over a terrible case of nerves just before the *Meistersinger* quintet by telling me precisely the same thing Strauss had said so many years earlier: "Just *be* Eva, think as Eva, and forget all about Lotte Lehmann. Just think this way: 'Hans Sachs wants me to make a speech. I don't quite know what I'm expected to do, I've never had to say anything quite that important in a formal context, and I wonder how I'm going to find the right words; but on the other hand, why should it be so hard? After all, I'm among friends. There is Sachs, whom I respect so highly. There is Walther von Stolzing, to whom my heart belongs. It ought to be easy to express such deep happiness.' " Meanwhile the music led me on, just as I was being led by my thoughts, so that I was able to begin the difficult, dreaded quintet in utter serenity. One should never relax onstage while others are singing; it is of the utmost importance to remain strictly within the personality of one's particular role throughout the performance. I remember how a colleague once remarked on my always seeming tense inside all the while I was onstage, even while I was not actually singing. "I don't work that way," he told me. "I use the respite to relax and recoup my strength for later on."

That, however, was never my custom, and I was very proud when Toscanini, after a *Tannhäuser* performance in New York, told me that he had been closely watching me all the time and had seen to his great delight that never for one moment did I forget to be Elisabeth.

Great praise, indeed, coming from so exalted and unforgettable a master.

Back, now, to *Die Frau ohne Schatten*.

The Wife, frowning, stands next to Barak. "I've been your wife now for two and a half years," she tells him. "I've still not conceived. Time for you to forget your ambitions."

Barak gets up and ties the skins into a bundle. Ignoring his Wife's black mood, he quietly tells her that he can never get really angry at her and that he knows her attitude will change when the day comes for which he is hoping and praying.

He pays no attention to her protests and leaves for the market, singing his ditty, to which she has had to listen so often that now it drives her to distraction: "If I carry the goods to market, I'll save on the donkey. . . ."

The Wife, sitting on a pile of skins, is alone, lost in somber reflections, when she hears a faint rustle in the air. There is a glaring flash of light, and suddenly the Empress and the Nurse are standing in the room, looking down at the frightened woman.

For the first time the Empress has come face to face with the harsh sight of poverty. Greatly confused, she looks about her, and suddenly in rapture her eyes light upon the long black shadow cast by the Dyer's Wife. Forgotten now is all the poverty about her; this woman possesses the one true fortune worth having, the one thing in the world she wants. The Empress casts an entreating glance in the direction of the Nurse, a silent question.

Now the Nurse is in her true element. Bowing deeply to the still frightened Dyer's Wife, making a gesture as though preparing to kiss her feet, she addresses her as though she were some exalted beauty, a mistress without peer. How, she inquires in feigned amazement, is it possible for such beauty to be confined in such humble surroundings? And who, if one might ask, was the hideous creature who just left the hut, an elderly man, short and squat—could he have been one of Her Ladyship's servants, the lowliest among the retinue?

Actually the Wife would not be inclined to disagree with the Nurse: Barak is, in fact, rather ugly and certainly no longer young; she is married to him, and ashamed of it. Yet once again the inner contradiction makes her defend her husband the instant he is attacked. Besides, her instinct warns her that this old woman is a deliberately deceitful flatterer. "You know very well who he was," she says. "He was Barak the Dyer. I am his Wife, and this is our home."

The Nurse, feigning stunned amazement, expresses indignation at the thought that a woman of such overweening beauty would marry so downright ugly a man. She goes on to praise the delicacy of the Wife's features, refers to her as a queen, and in the end succeeds in deeply troubling the woman, to whom no one has ever spoken in this manner. With icy terror in her heart, the Wife realizes that this uncanny creature before her, who suddenly appeared out of nowhere without crossing the doorstep, bears evil and deceit.

But the cunning Nurse knows all about the weaknesses of human beings and how to prey on them. She therefore pretends to be leaving, along with the Empress, who, still lost in the contemplation of the shadow, has stood aside. "Woe unto us, my child," the Nurse laments. "Woe unto us, and let us be gone. This one is turning us out and does not want our services. She knows the secret and will mock us. . . ."

The secret? What secret? Now the woman's curiosity is aroused; she wants to find out about the secret hidden behind the twitching forehead of the evil old woman, but her eager question is answered in a devious manner. "The secret of the purchase," the Nurse says in an aside highly charged with meaning, "the secret of the purchase and the secret of the price for which you can buy everything." The Dyer's Wife can make nothing of this; her poverty is such that she has nothing either to buy or to sell. Quickly, however, the Nurse points at the shadow: what about that? Would her shadow be of any great importance to Her Ladyship? Wouldn't she be rather happy to part with it, sell it at whatever price she wants to name, for everything or anything in the world?

The Wife, taken aback, does not understand; who on earth would want a shadow? Who would give even a single penny for one?

The Nurse believes the battle to be half won and proceeds to promise wealth beyond all imagining, conjures up the vision of lovers longing for the embrace of the gorgeous woman dressed in satin and silk. To prove her point, she claws the air and snatches out of it a magnificent diadem, which she hands to the Dyer's Wife. The woman holds it, speechless with delight; never in her life has she seen anything like it, not even in the wildest of the dreams in which she longed to escape the sordid misery of this hut. Gleefully triumphant, the Nurse at once dresses the Wife in precious brocade, and with a lax wave of her hand transmutes the hut into a fairy palace.

This particular scene was staged with striking effect in Vienna. A huge glass platform rose out of the pit, with girls in slave costumes on it; multicolored lights played on it from below, and the vision was absolutely ravishing. The transformation came about after the brief moment of darkness which had to suffice for my change of costume. Two helpers stood by, ready and waiting; they quickly wrapped me in a brocade coat and fastened the diadem in my hair. Every movement had been practiced to perfection, and my sudden reappearance as a "queen" must have been a rather impressive sight. A huge gold mirror was held up by the slave girls, and I stepped in front of it, kneeling slowly. Above it all rose the voice of the Nurse: "Will you not exchange your empty shadow for the splendor of this image?" And the voice of a youthful lover, one of the many promised by the Nurse, began its campaign of seductive flattery, singing: "For this image in the mirror I would give my soul, my life . . ."

The Dyer's Wife, faint and dizzy, feels as though she were dreaming and yet knows, at the same time, that it is all brilliant reality. Her ecstatic outcry makes the vision pale, and a moment later she stands there again as the poor Dyer's Wife.

Once again this involved a brief moment of darkness and a change of costumes accomplished in desperate haste. Somehow this race against time always came off without a hitch, but it invariably left me trembling from head to foot.

The Dyer's Wife, now violently impatient, is more than eager to find out just what she must do in order to trade her useless shadow for all this splendor. The Nurse gives her to understand that the shadow means motherhood, that to trade it away will lead to barrenness. She does not quite spell this out in so many words, but the Wife catches the general meaning.

Yet what does motherhood mean to her at this moment in her life? She is greedy for the vision of glamour she has just beheld, wants the diadem in her hair, the soft caressing feel of brocade around her shoulders. Motherhood? She had given up hope for that long ago, and now, on the spot, she decides that Barak never again will come close to her, that she never again will expose herself to the danger of bringing about the miracle of motherhood. Never another embrace. Never again.

She makes this vow, with the triumphant Nurse as witness.

The phrase "Thus I have spoken and sworn in my heart" was written by Strauss as though for a low contralto. When I asked him why he had done this, he laughed and told me that he was terribly fond of hearing a soprano singing at a lower pitch—not a true alto, that is, but the always somewhat strange sound of a high voice being forced to sing below its natural register. "Not every soprano has your unusual range," he added. "And every note has to be there, even if it is being whispered."

On that same occasion I asked him why he had written the part of Octavian in *Der Rosenkavalier* for a female voice. I remember how he looked at me in utter amazement. "Have you ever seen a man young enough to play Octavian and at the same time experienced enough to be an accomplished actor?" he asked. "Where would you find someone like that? Besides, writing for three sopranos was a challenge. I think I did the right thing."

I rather think so myself.

The Nurse now cajoles the Wife to cast motherhood away as something irksome, contemptible. But those are dangerous words, and something deep in the heart of the Dyer's Wife warns her to reconsider because love and motherhood *cannot* be contemptible. With a shudder she turns away, but once again the Nurse demonstrates her cunning. "O rare one, O ruler, O queen," she says, and the feigned deference blinds the Dyer's Wife to the truth evoked by her own conscience. She wants to be different from the other women around her, those perpetual breeders whom until now she secretly has envied for their hordes of children. To be different, to rise above the miseries of a humdrum existence, of a poverty-ridden life—isn't that a worthy ambition? And her sacrifice is going to be well rewarded . . . No, no more Barak, whom she hates precisely because she is forced to love him in spite of herself.

With hidden horror she watches as the Nurse mumbles the magic formulas that will tangle her in the web and put her within the old woman's power. For the next three days these two creatures from the spirit world will be living here in this hut of hers, as required by the magic spell. And at the end of that period the Wife must wittingly and with deliberate intent surrender her shadow and trade it in exchange for all the world's glamour. But upon hearing the words "surrender her shadow," the Dyer's Wife shivers in sudden fright. Was it really, truly right of her to make such a promise? Is it going to be worth the things she will receive in exchange? But the canny Nurse, aware of the Wife's inner conflict, immediately proceeds to paint visions of splendor for the benefit of the reluctant woman, visions of infinite joy, infinite wealth of both objects and experience.

Hearing her husband's footfall, the Wife bids the Nurse to be silent. Barak is coming home from work, and she has no meal waiting for him. What is more, she will have to refuse herself to him. But once again the Nurse is ready with help and good advice: starting tomorrow, she whispers to the Dyer's Wife, they will come here disguised as poor relatives who want to work as servants. This is what she is to tell her husband. They'll be helping her and be around all the time except for a brief period in the middle of each night which no one needs to know about.

Once again the Dyer's Wife reacts with a shudder; these nocturnal voyages smack of black magic, and the inner struggle consumes her as she stands immobile, petrified, unable to make up her mind. But black magic, if that is what it is, comes in good stead, for now fish are flying through the air and landing in a pan all ready on the hearth, which flares up suddenly with a lively fire. In the back of the room Barak's bed, which for the past two and a half years has stood next to that of his Wife, suddenly slides away and disappears, moved by invisible hands, and both the Nurse and the Empress vanish in an equally silent and mysterious manner.

[46]

The Dyer's Wife, left alone and exhausted, collapses on a bundle of skins. Was all this a dream? The unimaginable glamour, the glory of the palace, the diadem in her hair? Limp and rigid with fright, she is trying to remember it all when suddenly the whimpering cries of small voices shatter her dream. They seem to be coming straight out of the flames, crying: "Mother, Mother, we're in darkness and in fear. Mother, Mother, let us come home to you. Woe unto us, you've hardened your heart. . . ."

Writhing in horror, the Dyer's Wife realizes that these are the voices of her own children, her unborn children, whom she is ready to give up for the sake of vain glamour, children willed by her to die before they have been born.

At this moment, Barak is coming back, humming the same ditty that she has come to hate so much. "If I carry the goods to market, I'll save on the donkey. . . ."

A harmless enough song, of which Barak is very fond; but now it brings back to his Wife all the humiliating misery of her everyday existence, the uncouth and unimaginative husband smugly content to be what he is, the joyless routine of toil and trouble. Once again she feels right about trading this for the glamour of a magic world filled with beauty. Without so much as acknowledging her husband's greetings, she turns silently away from him and moves to the back of the room. He sees the fish in the skillet and exclaims over the good meal his Wife has prepared for him; but when he asks her to join him, she suddenly tells him to go ahead and eat by himself whenever he feels like it. His bed, moreover, has been moved; from now on he is to sleep on the other side of the room because some cousins of hers are to start working for her as servants and will sleep at the foot of her bed.

And with a vehement gesture she shuts the curtain that conceals her bed.

Barak, profoundly hurt, sits down on the floor and starts

to nibble on a piece of old bread he finds in his pocket: he has lost his appetite for whatever she had made for him. The fish go on sizzling to no purpose.

He has been told that pregnant women are likely to act in a bizarre and unpredictable fashion, and he comforts himself with that bit of hand-me-down wisdom. But it is hard for him just the same, and the food turns sour in his mouth.

Night has fallen. The night watchmen outside are making their rounds, singing their evening song:

> You couples lovingly embracing,
> You are the bridge that spans the abyss
> Across which the dead return to life.
> Blessed be the fruit of your love.

His Wife has nothing further to say to Barak, and like a heavy cloud the slowly descending curtain covers the tragic vision of lonely and errant human beings.

I am proud to recall the truly extraordinary way in which this opera was staged in Vienna. Alfred Roller had outdone himself, and each of the roles was performed by the ideal singer. There was Maria Jeritza as the Empress, towering and beautiful. Karl Aagard-Oestvig was a marvelous and majestic Emperor. Richard Mayr, beloved and never to be forgotten, sang Barak the Dyer; the dark, heartwarming timbre of his voice still resounds in my ears and will never be effaced.

The Nurse was originally sung by the excellent Lucy Weidt, but later on in almost all performances by Bella Paalen who made this exceedingly difficult role her very own. She sang all of its tortuous complexities with the greatest ease, and acted the demoniac old woman in a horrifyingly realistic manner. The role of the Dyer's Wife, which I sang at the world premiere, occasionally was taken over by the great singing actress Marie Gutheil-Schoeder, but I was delighted whenever I had a chance to sing it, even when I realized that the vocal requirements of the role were almost exceeding my limitations.

Last but not least we had Franz Schalk as conductor, and as always I felt wholly one with him.

Strauss himself also frequently conducted, and later on Clemens Krauss took the baton, bringing with him an entire new team of singers. The Empress was now sung by Viorica Ursuleac, who was later to marry Krauss, the Nurse by Gertrud Rünger, the Emperor by Franz Völker, and the Dyer by Josef von Manowarda. For some reason I retained my former role.

I should like here to say a few words about my relations with Clemens Krauss.

My behavior toward him was not, I am afraid, marked by excessive moderation and understanding. Now that the bitterness in my heart has had time to settle, it seems to me that I should have been able to appreciate the basic truth that every new conductor will quite naturally sponsor his own favorite team of singers. He is expected to come up with new plans and new ideas, and only my own passionate devotion to Schalk can have blinded me to this obvious fact. I fiercely opposed Krauss when, with just a slight effort on my part, we might have become good friends. As it was, all I saw in him was the man who had usurped Schalk's place and who was determined always to hand the best roles to his intimate friend Viorica Ursulcac. We often tend to act on foolish impulses, when with a bit of goodwill we could easily see the other person's point of view and replace animosity by understanding.

As for Krauss, he seemed genuinely surprised at my open hostility, and I can scarcely blame him. Now that I am sufficiently remote from it all and able to view both myself and our relationship with a measure of objective detachment, I feel sorry that we never had a chance to have it out in the open and discuss the whole situation with candor and sincerity. Too late.

At any rate, he was an excellent conductor, specializing in the music of Richard Strauss. He was the composer's most devoted friend, and if my name ever was mentioned between them, I can imagine Strauss, eyebrows raised and mouth twisted in a mocking smile, saying: "God protect me from those idiotic sopranos. What do you want, Lehmann is eating her heart out because there are other sopranos in the world besides her."

And in this he would have been wrong.

It is worth here recounting an incident that proved Krauss's profound grasp of the artist's mentality. At a performance of *Die Frau ohne Schatten* during the Salzburg Festival, Pauline Strauss insulted me most outrageously during the intermission between the first and second acts. She made an unfortunate remark of a purely personal nature which with the best will in the world I could not excuse on the grounds of her well-known temper. I was in a state near collapse and felt incapable of going on. Weeping, I pulled off my wig and started getting out of my costume. Everyone around me was duly horrified. Strauss, Krauss, Lothar Wallerstein, and many others begged me to be reasonable and to go on singing.

I screamed at them all to get out and leave me alone. I did not want to see anybody, and I was not going to go on. Finished.

Thereupon Krauss decided to take a desperate chance. He had judged me correctly, and he won the game. Calmly ascending the dais, he began to conduct the opening to the second act.

The strains of the familiar music brought me around at once. In great haste I slapped the wig back on my disheveled hair, wiggled into my costume, raced out onto the stage, and stood there as the curtain rose, tears streaming down my face and into the daring décolleté. But there I was, driven by instinct, by the inner compulsion characteristic of the true performer that the show must go on. It would have given me great pleasure to slap Krauss's grinning face because I was furious with him for having shown such an astute and accurate appreciation of both my strength and my weakness. But now that it is too late, I would like to salute him for it.

Incidentally, Pauline really had meant well; it was just that she had a most unfortunate way of expressing her opinions. The next day Strauss sent me flowers—a truly extraordinary gesture, considering his customary reticence—along with a note explaining that it was only her great love for me that had made Pauline so specially demanding where I was concerned. And so peace reigned once again.

Act Two

The following morning. Again Barak is about to take his wares to market. His Wife, seated on a bundle of skins, impatiently waits for him to be off. A kerchief covers her jet-black hair, but beneath it she can feel the pearls and diamonds pinned there by the Nurse. She can hardly wait to admire her new and disturbing beauty in the mirror.

The Nurse follows Barak outside, imploring him not to be gone too long because his poor Wife is so very lonesome without him and consumed by longing. Barak looks at her quietly; he obviously does not like this strange old woman, who in so mysterious a manner has managed to insinuate herself into their lives. He leaves, with one last fond look at his Wife, who pays no attention to him.

The Nurse now heaves a sigh of relief. The time has come. With the predatory grace of a wildcat, she slinks over to where the Wife is sitting, and deferentially asks if she should now call for the man of her dreams.

The Dyer's Wife either does not understand or does not

want to. The Nurse, however, cunningly insists that there must be someone, some secret passion. Is there really no one other than her hideous husband?

The Dyer's Wife shakes her head. No one, she maintains, lives in her vacant heart, and she is dressing up for no one but the mirror.

The omniscient old woman leans over her with an evil cackle. "Really?" she asks. "What about the one who appeared to you in your dreams, the one you saw but once, in passing, and whose image has yet haunted you ever since? . . ."

The Dyer's Wife begins to shake and tremble. Yes, she did dream of one whom she neither knows nor will come to know, one much dearer to her heart than Barak. But how is it possible for this mysterious old woman to divine the innermost secrets of her heart, to read her mind? Turning to the Nurse, she gives herself away by her own question, and the old woman gleefully promises to summon the one who is thus making her heart ache in sweet anguish.

Once more the young woman gives herself away because she cannot believe that this Nurse or whatever she may be possibly could know something that she herself never has really owned up to. After all, it was but a single time that she saw him, out in the street . . . very young, handsome, almost a boy . . . and thereafter only in her dreams.

Furtively, in the meantime, the Nurse has taken hold of a broomstick and made it assume the shape of this boy. The kettle, in turn, is ordered to speak in the boy's voice.

The Empress, quietly forgotten in the corner, watches with growing horror and outrage. These, then, are human beings, so easily bought, seduced, corrupted. She is humiliated by her part in this terrifying game, but realizes that it is being played for her sake and salvation.

A beautiful youth suddenly materializes, limp as though unconscious, almost lifeless, just having crossed the line from the realm of the spirits.

Slowly he lifts his arms toward the Dyer's Wife, and she in turn, as though in a trance, approaches him with hesitant step. Suddenly the Empress screams in terror—Barak is returning. Clairvoyant, she has seen him on his way. The Nurse covers the youth with a scrap of fur, the stage is briefly dimmed, and when the lights come on again the broom rests in a corner as before.

The Wife stands, stunned. Barak is coming back, bringing with him a whole crowd of people. Business was good today. He sold all his skins and has money enough to treat his neighbors to a feast. The children all dance around him, singing and crying with joy.

His Wife, however, looks at the happy scene with hate-filled eyes. Her dream, her sweet, secret dream was about to come true, and now these intruders have destroyed it. Disappointment and helpless rage make her break out in tears.

Barak watches her, sadly resigned, inviting the neighbors to help themselves to food and drink, and tells them to pay no attention to his Wife. Her tongue is sharp, but actually she is a good-hearted woman.

The Empress is profoundly moved by Barak's nobility and kindness. She finds him magnificent in his forthright simplicity, deserving of a kinder fate, whereas his happiness is being wrecked through her own actions.

Barak asks her to bring his Wife some food, something good and sweet. She obeys readily enough, but is chased away by harsh words of his Wife, and flees in sudden fear because no one has ever talked this way to her before; the shrill ugly words cut like whiplashes. Trembling, she retires into a corner.

The others all praise Barak and are determined to disregard his Wife. "Oh, day of happiness," they start their song, while the Dyer's Wife, crying, pursues her own lament: "The brute will inherit the earth, and I shall have nothing left but my tears."

The following scene opens in the forest cottage where the

Empress and the Nurse are to spend these three nights in accord with the terms of the magic spell. It also requires them to keep silent about the plan and, above all, not to let the Emperor in on the scheme. The Empress therefore has sent him a message informing him that for three days the cottage will be her refuge, that she wants to spend the time in quiet contemplation far from the world. Guileless, he has accepted the message, but the white falcon has led him to the cottage. Now he is waiting at the door, silent and tense, not knowing even what it is that he is waiting for. He senses the vast emptiness within and wonders why his wife would have lied to him, but as he sees her and the Nurse arrive in silence, he hides in the shadows, senses the breath of human beings upon them, and realizes that she has deceived him deliberately.

Lamenting his fate, he decides that his honor commands him to kill her. But how? He could not use the arrow, the same arrow that once upon a time was meant for the white gazelle and at whose touch she became his wife. What about the sword? With a stroke of that same sword he had undone her belt; how could he now run it through her beloved body? Is he, then, to choke her with his hands, hands that touched and caressed her? Never will they kill that which their touch awakened to sweet life.

Desperate, the Emperor wanders off, seeking solitude.

This particular aria is entrancingly beautiful, written in long and swinging phrases, its warm, replete melody marking the transition from this scene to the next.

The next scene is frequently omitted. In a sense, I admit, it is indeed a repetition of the scene at the Dyer's house, yet I consider it to be of very great importance. It shows the Dyer's Wife being haunted and harassed, driven into the fine-meshed net cunningly spun by the evil Nurse. But invariably, at the very last second, already teetering at the brink, she resists temptation, rejects seduction, and offers highly significant clues as to the true force of her character. Step by step she frees herself from her hatred of Barak and gradually emerges as his loving Wife, the very person that in her heart of hearts she has been all along.

As the curtain rises, she stands off to one side, casting dark looks in Barak's direction, impatient for him to be off because she is eager to wear her pearls and her diadem. Barak, however, is in no hurry today; he feels tired, it has been a hot day, and he has done little work. With few skins to sell, he would in any case be back from market soon; and so the Nurse mixes a sleeping draught with the water he requests.

The Dyer immediately falls asleep, and his Wife looks down on him with ineffable contempt. At this moment she hates him more than ever before, and savagely she lights into him with reproaches and accusations which, because he is already fast asleep, he cannot hear.

The Nurse finally drags her away and tells her about the sleeping draught: "He'll sleep till tomorrow."

Yet the Nurse, who knows all about good and evil, is profoundly ignorant when it comes to the human heart and cannot even begin to understand the Wife now anxiously bending over her husband, fearing for his health and worrying lest harm befall him. Secret lovers? The Dyer's Wife flares up in righteous anger. No one is to enter this house of hers, no one summoned by the Nurse, that is. If he were really the Master of her Dreams, her true love, she would be calling him herself, and he would obey *her* orders and wishes rather than those of the Nurse.

Hearing this, the Nurse in sudden triumph calls out, and that very instant the startled, terrified Dyer's Wife, confronts the beautiful creature who has ruled her dreams.

Hofmannsthal gave the following stage directions: "The youth had best be represented by a dancer, either male or female, turning his back to the public, while the singer is to be posted in the prompter's box, so that his song issues forth in ethereal and ghostly detachment."

I remember Toni Birkmayer, so enchantingly beautiful as the youth that no one could have blamed the Dyer's Wife for taking him as her lover.

She, however, is reluctant and undecided. Feeling irresistibly drawn to the beautiful creature, she reaches toward him with a sensuous gesture, and whispers as though in a dream: "I dreamed of flying to you with ceaseless kisses, like a turtle-dove feeding its brood—and my dream has killed you. . . ."

The youth swoons upon hearing her words, and she gazes down upon his inert form longingly. The moment has come, and the Nurse hastily tries to drag the guilt-ridden Empress away from the scene. But as the Wife comes to realize that the women want to leave her alone, want to afford her the opportunity to sin and to ally herself in sinning to the two creatures whom she hates and despises, she leaps up with a wild scream, away from the form at her feet.

Desperately shaking Barak, she finally succeeds in rousing him from his drugged sleep. "Wake up, wake up," she cries. "Help me—there is a man in the house." And while Barak painfully collects himself, the Nurse hastily flings her coat over the youth, muttering under her breath: "God protect us from childish idiots." The Empress, on the other hand, has assisted the Dyer's Wife in the laborious struggle to rouse Barak. A burning conflict tears her heart assunder; she wants the Nurse's wiles to succeed for her own sake, but she cannot bear to witness the corruption that she has helped to spawn.

Once Barak is fully awake, his Wife can only scold and curse him. Fool that he is, what business does he have to fall asleep like this? He is supposed to be wide awake and taking care of his Wife. One more trick like this and she certainly will leave him.

Yet despite his sadness he senses that she did miss him, that in spite of her harsh words she wants him here, by her side. Sadly he gazes upon his tools. "I don't know what's been happening to me," he complains. "I'm being toyed with by the powers of darkness; my very best mortar has sprung a crack —don't I know my own trade anymore?"

His trade is his bread, and not his alone. His work must provide for his Wife and his Brothers, for many of the neighbors' children. And soon now there may be a child of his own to relish the fruits of his labor. Hence he is worried. "The powers of darkness . . ." He senses their presence without knowing anything about them.

The Wife is indignant. Here this fool worries about his work, his broken mortar, when the tenuous link between them almost snapped in her desire to embrace the beautiful youth. Her senses drove her toward sin, but in her heart something held her back, told her that she must remain Barak's alone.

She acknowledges this feeling with a kind of stubborn reluctance. But at the same time a change has come over her, brought about by the realization that he never will really understand her and that there is no point in making sacrifices for someone like him, forever unaware. Inwardly shaking, she turns on him with sullen irony. "There is one trade you most certainly know nothing about," she says. "Never did, and never will. Otherwise you wouldn't carry on about that silly mortar of yours." Good heavens, if he only knew how close she had come to the brink, how at the very last instant she had drawn back, rushed to him for protection. And what does she get in return? Like a donkey he plods on along the very edge of the precipice, never even aware of the gaping abyss at his side, let alone the mysteries in its depths.

Barak turns to the Empress kneeling by his side and helping him collect his tools. He simply cannot understand what has come over him; a strange sort of darkness is troubling his mind, and he worries about not being able to feed those who depend on him.

The Wife laughs out loud. "Don't you be worrying about food . . ." She'll be gone from this miserable hovel, she'll walk along beautiful gardens, in the spacious and airy quarters of the rich, down in the city where perhaps one day she will again meet the beautiful youth face to face. And perhaps, one day, she will stay away for good, never to return; for after all, she is not like a bird that Barak bought in the market. She is free, at home in other realms where no one dares to follow. And, by way of challenge, she flings a bright kerchief over her shoulders and walks off, laughing.

The Nurse follows her, but the Empress remains with Barak. Though not seeing her, he is aware of a creature who wishes him well, and to his question she answers gently and quietly: "It is I, my Lord, your servant."

The next scene takes place in the Empress's chamber at the forest cottage. She is reclining on her bed, with the Nurse seated at her feet. Nightmares torment her slumber. She has visions of Barak, his wildly desperate eyes imploring her help. "It's all my fault, Barak," she cries out in her sleep, but Barak's image pales. And now the Emperor approaches the threshold of this place destined to become his tomb unless his wife can find a shadow. His falcon circles above his head, emitting plaintive, pitiful cries, as though wanting to hold him back and stay the hand of fate. But the Emperor insists on going ahead, to seek his doom.

All this is part of the Empress's dream. Waking abruptly, she shudders and sighs, torn between her duty to save the man she loves and her guilt at wanting to destroy the noble, innocent Dyer.

"Whatever I touch," she wails, "dies under my hands. Woe unto me. Would that I myself were to turn to stone." And on this desperate outcry the curtain drops.

The role of the Empress is a magnificent one. Maria Jeritza, the incomparable Empress of our world premiere, recently wrote an article about it in a magazine, and I am sure that she will permit me to quote here what Richard Strauss said when he asked her to accept this role rather than that of the Dyer's Wife, which—as she asserts—originally had been meant for her. "Your real triumph," he said, "begins with the third act and grows in scope all the way to the end." This is very true. It took a superb actress to highlight the role in such a way as to indicate its crucial importance right from the very beginning, when the Empress actually has very little singing to do, but must be able to move the audience by the sheer force of her acting. And in that Maria Jeritza succeeded.

The Dyer's Wife, on the other hand, all but kills herself singing throughout every single scene, while the Empress gradually unfolds not only her voice but her whole being in the course of the second half of the opera, a situation that allows her to reap the lion's share of the laurels. Jeritza knew perfectly well what she was doing when she decided on this role rather than that of the Dyer's Wife, but the more I think back to those childish rivalries of long ago, the more I approve of Strauss's decision to switch the roles. For I was not the type to weigh roles on the scale of individual effects; a purely personal success was not part of my ambition in those blessed days when team spirit prevailed. I was perfectly content to sing myself into a state of near prostration and then gradually fade out toward the end.

Strauss, knowing both of us very well, had made a wise decision.

In the following scene we return to the Dyer's hut on a dark and gloomy day dense with gathering clouds. Barak, seated on the floor, is unable to get started on his work and soon is joined by his Brothers, who drift back into the hut, impelled by some ineffable fear. Even the Nurse, standing in the back of the room, seems uneasy. "Supernatural powers have taken a hand," she senses, quaking with fright. Still, she plans her strategy so as to counteract these interventions; she will call on the Power of Evil and thus make her plan succeed after all. The Empress, lost in melancholy admiration of Barak's unchanging kindness, pays no attention to her. All the other human beings she has seen have been victims of their own greed; he alone has shown her the true significance of the word "man," a being risen above the level of animals, striving toward greatness and goodness. "For his sake I shall remain among people, breathe their breath and share their sorrow. . ." These feelings make the Empress vacillate, shake her decision to save her husband regardless of the consequences.

The Dyer's Wife, however, is assailed by darker thoughts. The day oppresses her, disaster seems to loom, and fear has gripped her by the throat. She wants to get away, to flee this miserable hut which has seen nothing but heartbreak. She casts a mean glance at Barak, always even-tempered, kind, and soft-spoken. Is there no way at all to shake this creature out of his indifference, his equanimity, his provocative even-tempered goodness, which is driving her out of her mind? She does not listen to his sad words, does not hear the terror in his voice, does not sense the burden on his mind. She hardly can draw a breath in this sweltering heat. She needs air. Rising abruptly, against the background of a sky torn by lightning and the ominous rumble of thunder, she savagely rails at Barak, hurls wild accusations at him. Nothing, she screams, nothing can touch him. He is like an animal shuttling from pallet to trough and from trough to pallet, with no other thought in the world. She despises him, and he deserves her contempt, every bit of it—people who act like cattle should be treated like cattle. He does not own her. Never did, and never will. While he was away peddling his wares, she entertained lovers right here in this hut, gave herself to them, and was still warm with their kisses when he got home.

Barak does not seem to be hearing her at all. Motionless, he squats on the ground, the torrent of words pouring over him like a raging river that has burst its dikes. His passive suffering, his determined refusal to hit back at her, drives the Wife into ever more savage paroxysms of rage. She wants him to listen. She wants him to hear every word of what she has to say. The three Brothers are howling like madmen, the storm shakes the rickety cottage and threatens to wreck it at any moment, but her fury continues unabated. "Shut them up," she orders. "I want you to hear me."

She does not want others to make fun of him, she explains. She wants him to know exactly what it is that she has done. Three days running she welcomed a lover while he was away. But then, with a gesture of despair, she rears up and turns on him in a new outburst of fury: "But the joy of it was poisoned at the source because I had to think of you, the very one I wanted to forget, and your face appeared to me when I least wanted to see it." This is the only true statement among all her wild tales. Uttering it, she almost faints away. Rousing herself once again, she viciously tells Barak that at long last she has found a way to forget him. Hands uplifted, she stands in the middle of the room and utters the blasphemous curse. "My womb shall bear no fruit, neither to you nor to anyone else." Thus she will be freed of all restraints, cut loose from Barak. Free, like the wind and the clouds. That was why she sold her shadow, and the price now is within her grasp.

With growing horror Barak listens to her harangue and finally rises, a powerful figure of wrath, cutting her short. "This woman is insane," he cries. "Light a fire and let me see her face." The fire flares up, and there stands his Wife in the middle of the room, casting no shadow. Barak staggers back. Gone are his gentleness, his understanding, his willingness to forgive. He is all judge now, passing sentence upon this woman, who has dared not only to betray him but also to announce her betrayal with triumph in her voice. He will have to kill her, drown her in the river. And at that very moment a strange miracle occurs, for from somewhere above a sword drops into his hand. Barely restrained by his frightened Brothers, Barak advances toward his Wife.

With devilish glee the Nurse has been watching the scene; she now urges the Empress in a loud whisper to snatch the shadow quickly. The magic spells requires that the Empress herself complete the job. Here, then, within her grasp is salvation, the shadow that no longer belongs to anyone. She must take it, quickly.

But the Empress turns away. "I don't want the shadow," she cries out, with sudden determination. "It is sullied by blood, and I will not touch it. I shall not have the blood of human beings on my hands."

The Dyer's Wife, meanwhile, has watched Barak's transformation in speechless terror. For the first time she now sees the real man underneath, the man about to pass judgment on her at the very moment when she herself is undergoing a similar transformation. For now that she recognizes the lord and master in him, her half-buried love for him breaks through like a dammed-up, all-powerful torrent, and she gives herself over to his death blow as to the supreme embrace.

Music of ineffable beauty carries this scene of recognition and rebirth. The Wife's voice breaks like a ray of sunlight through the ominous darkness, and the confession of her lie is rendered in a melody whose magic purity still makes my heart beat faster whenever I think of it.

Barak seems unyielding, relentless. Too deep the wound that has been struck; the sword in his hand flashes, raised for the death blow. But quite as abruptly as it appeared, the weapon is snatched from his hand, the blow stayed by magic powers. The cottage shakes, the earth opens, and a sudden flood swamps them all. Barak and his Wife go under; his Brothers barely manage to float out through the door and save themselves.

The Nurse helps the Empress to a higher part of the wall. Darkness is complete, and only the Nurse's voice is heard, accusing and invoking supernatural powers.

Thus the second act ends.

I must confess frankly that I never have been very fond of the tortuously elaborate libretto. To follow the intricate plot of this opera is impossible without considerable homework ahead of time. People have told me time and again that they find the music truly divine—"But what, in heaven's name, is the story all about?" That, in my opinion, is why *Die Frau ohne Schatten* will never enjoy great popularity.

Still, the music is indescribably beautiful. It speaks a language all its own, simply overwhelming, and really requires no help from any medium other than itself.

Personally I very much enjoyed singing the Dyer's Wife once I had mastered both the libretto and the music. I grew oblivious to the vocal difficulties and chose to disregard the fact that it is the Empress who, at the end, is handed the choice triumph of the individual performer.

The staging, which involves fantastically quick changes, used to present the producer with a series of staggering problems. At the 1932 Salzburg Festival we were giving *Die Frau ohne Schatten*, and staging this grandiose opera in the smaller Festival House proved to be a task of extraordinary complexity. I shall never forget our dress rehearsal, at which just about everything went wrong. The scene changes never were ready on time, and the strain and excitement pushed all of us close to the brink of nervous breakdown.

The most desperate of the lot was our producer, Lothar

Wallerstein. On the night of the performance, I saw him fervently making the sign of the cross. "I'm a Jew, of course," he explained, with an almost absentminded look in his eyes. "But I figured it couldn't hurt, and it might help."

It did.

We gave a magnificent performance, once again reaffirming the old show business superstition about dress rehearsals and premieres; the worse the rehearsal, the better the opening.

But we paid for it with our nerves.

Act Three

Act III opens with a wonderful duet between Barak and his Wife. Richard Mayr used to sing his part so divinely that I shall never cease regretting that it was not recorded and preserved for posterity. Our voices blended well, and whenever I sang with him, I had a feeling that my voice was being carried by his on velvet wings.

As the curtain rises, the Dyer and his Wife are near one another and yet far apart, imprisoned in an underground cave and separated by a thick wall. Neither knows anything about the other. The Wife, tearful, is wringing her hands in despair, hearing the voices of her unborn children.

"Be silent," she implores them. "I haven't done it."

And in the beautiful duet she goes on to tell of her longing for her husband, her passionate desire to bear his children, her desperate hope to be forgiven, to hear one word of understanding from his lips.

Barak in turn feels guilty for having blindly believed his Wife's false confession of adultery. He, whose task it was to guard her, save her from misfortune, instead brought down upon her the most horrible disasters. She, too, will be consumed by loneliness just as it is consuming him in ten thousand torments.

Suddenly he is caught in a ray of light, and an angel's voice bids him leave the cave. On the other side of the wall, the same thing happens to the Wife; the angel of light is delivering them both, and they rush off, frantically searching for one another.

Here the scene ends, and I have heard people ask in utter bewilderment how an angel possibly could deliver them when they had been led to believe that Keikobad had full power over their fate.

I would like to offer my own explanation. Keikobad thought that his daughter would detest the human race just as he himself did. He had been certain that his own child, able to stand in the sun without casting a black shadow, would be repelled at the very idea of turning into a woman, and that she never could bear to be anything but transparent as glass. Never a wife, never a mother.

He had taken if for granted that she would leave the Emperor, even at the risk of having her beloved husband turn to stone, rather than have so despicable a fate befall her. She, however, saw that, quite on the contrary, human beings can be good and pure; and after Barak gave her proof of it, she refused to destroy him even to save her beloved.

Thus Keikobad lost, his power overcome by the greater power of love, the compassionate, all-embracing love for human beings. And he, Lord of the Spirit World, is big enough to understand this. If his daughter has decided to become a human being, he wants to see her human in the noblest and most exalted sense of the word. One final cruel test lies ahead of her, but if she persists in her determination, he will not only resign himself to it but help her as well.

For Keikobad is proud and just rather than cruel.

In the preceding scene, when Barak's house was destroyed,

the Nurse and the Empress saved themselves by climbing onto a high wall. A boat now suddenly appears at their feet, and, as they clamber aboard, it takes off at once on a course set by fate—by Keikobad.

The stage now is transformed into one vast shore, with the boat drifting toward it while the Nurse tries in vain to head it back out into the open water. She knows that this is the gateway to Keikobad's palace and fears his vengeance upon her beloved Empress, familiar as she believes herself to be with his cruelty.

The Empress, who had been asleep in the vessel, now sits up and with growing excitement notices the tall portals to the palace, the very ones that had appeared to her in the terrible nightmare she still is trying to shake off. In this nightmare she saw her husband stride to his doom through these same portals, and now she will enter them herself, confront her father, ask him to listen, understand, and judge.

The frightened Nurse tries to dissuade her; Keikobad, she insists, is cruel enough to destroy his own child. She truly loves the Empress and wants to drag her away by cajolery or threats, but the Empress now feels certain that her place is by the side of her husband, and she is prepared to share his fate in death as well as in life. With open eyes she enters the gate, whose portals swing wide for her. "Our deeds shall judge us. The call of the heart shall summon us," she tells the unhappy old Nurse, bidding her good-bye forever because she wants to belong to the human race, which she has come to understand and to love.

This whole scene simply is one fantastic aria for the Empress, who can now tower in triumph over all the others who worked so vary hard in this opera merely to do their duty. Now she rules in lone splendor.

Maria Jeritza was devastatingly effective in this scene. Her voice had a marvelous golden sound, and her acting, as always, was commanding and wholly controlled. Bella Paalen, who—as I already mentioned—used to sing the Nurse, once asked Richard Strauss during a rehearsal if he had arranged the score purposely in such a way that she would have to scream herself to death and all but ruin her voice, at which precise point the Empress would come on to sing the most beautiful tune in the whole opera. Strauss laughed. "Of course," he affirmed. "That was precisely my intention. The Empress should rise here like a fountain of gold, and it's the Nurse's job to prepare for this."

"In that case," replied Bella Paalen, "let me thank you here and now in the name of all Nurses. You are indeed the mezzo-soprano's greatest friend and benefactor, and we shall erect a monument to you in our hearts."

Strauss was very fond of humor. He displayed almost alarmingly childish amusement when I once told him a funny story in Hamburg dialect. Let me add that my imitation of the Hamburg vernacular was rather crude and the joke itself reasonably pointless; still, he laughed until tears were streaming down his cheeks, and he made me repeat the story over and over until I came to dread mere mention of "that story about Erna and how she went down to the cellar to get some wine." I desperately searched my memory for some slightly more intelligent joke, but somehow "little Erna" had tickled his sense of humor, and time and again made him laugh just as though he never had heard it before.

This, however, has led us far afield from the somber miracle of *Die Frau ohne Schatten*.

Abandoned by the Empress, the portals shut in her face, the Nurse now calls down death and destruction upon the world and all mankind. To Barak, who appears while searching for his Wife, she points out the wrong way, and then repeats this act of spite when the Wife appears in turn. Thus the two stumble about, never guessing how close they are to one another.

In a wild surge of fear, the Nurse now calls upon Keikobad, but only his messenger appears, the one who delivered the original message and the three-day ultimatum. This time, however, he curtly bids her leave the threshold of the Mighty One. "Your fate will be to wander among the human race, to share the lives of those whom you despise, to mingle your breath with theirs, over and over." That is to be her sentence, passed by Keikobad because she had shown herself incapable of bending the Empress to his will. With a savage oath the Nurse collapses in the boat. "Fire eating into your bones . . ." is her final adieu as, amidst thunder and lightning, the boat drifts away.

Once again the scene changes. We hear the voices of Barak and his Wife, desperately calling one another. Slowly the stage lights up. Curtained off in the background of a vast, temple-like hall is a mysterious dark niche which the Empress slowly approaches, to the accompaniment of violins. "Father, are you there?" she asks. "Are you threatening me out of the recesses of darkness? Here, look down upon me, your own child. I have learned to give of myself, but I did not buy a shadow. Now show me the place that shall be mine among those who cast shadows."

Never, never shall I forget the voice of Jeritza as, emerging out of the violin music, it reached the very pinnacle of purity, as clear a sound as that of any violin. This scene brings back some of the most intensely beautiful memories of my whole life.

A golden fountain suddenly cascades out of the ground. But the Empress draws back from it. She does not want the waters of life, because she already has something more precious; love will bring her either life or death, and either life or death will be welcome for the sake of love.

A youth stands at the fountain, the guardian of the portals. "Drink, drink," he invites her, "and the shadow that once was that of the Dyer's Wife shall be yours, and you will be like her." Is it Keikobad who is thus tempting her? The Empress does not know, but she will not drink of the life-giving water because it would doom both Barak and his Wife. She cannot bring herself to send them to their death in order to save her own life and that of the Emperor.

The fountain stops as suddenly as it erupted, and she now demands to see her father. "I want my sentence," she insists. "Show me your face, Father."

A light suddenly dawns within the curtained niche, and through the gauze veil she now to her horror perceives not her father but her husband, seated on a refulgent throne, petrified, with only his eyes still imploring and alive.

This terribly exciting scene requires enormous means of expression. Strauss here suddenly makes the Empress *speak;* and no song could exceed in dramatic effect this outcry of a haunted creature tormented by guilt. For it had been well within her means to save her beloved husband; one sip from the life-giving waters would have brought him back to her alive and warm, would have helped her forget that others in his stead were consigned to doom.

"Woe unto you, O stars, that thus you do unto men," the Empress moans, flinging herself on the ground in wild despair. Slowly the statue recedes into darkness while the voice of the falcon rings out with the incantation: "The woman casts no shadow, and the Emperor shall turn to stone." Once more the fountain rises, spouting its stream of gold. "Say the word," the youth urges, enticing her. "Just say that you will drink of these waters, and the woman's shadow shall be yours. Your husband will rise, alive, and leave with you. Have just one sip . . ." This alluring voice is counterpointed by those of Barak and his Wife, plaintive and distant. "Dying . . . Have

[69]

mercy . . . dying . . . no help . . . woe unto us . . . dying."
The Empress, near exhaustion, once more rejects temptation in
a voice barely above a whisper. "Do not tempt me, Keikobad,"
she says. "I am your child. Let me die ere I succumb." And
slowly, swaying, she rises, stands next to the fountain of life,
and just barely has strength enough to call out, "I will not."

Abruptly the fountain dies. There is an instant of total darkness, and, as the hall lights up slowly, a dark shadow appears
at the feet of the Empress.

Slowly the Emperor rises and descends the steps of the
throne; he had been told that a pure heart breaking would
have the power to save him.

The Empress's heart, pure and translucent like a crystal,
broke in her final outcry. And a power far above that of
Keikobad now has given her the shadow she refused to acquire
by corruption. The voices of angels surround them, the voices
of unborn children now about to receive the gift of life. The
trial of these two is over; they have passed it and been re-
deemed by it. Like Tamino and Pamina they are about to
enter a realm in which purity and truth reign supreme. The
Emperor and Empress embrace while golden clouds conceal
the new change of scene.

As they recede, we see a beautiful landscape, with a water-
fall in the middle. Barak and his Wife face each other across
the torrent, and, as their eyes meet, a shadow springs up at
the Wife's feet, bridging the water, and the voices of their
children yet unborn rise in jubilation. They rush into each
other's arms across a golden bridge that now miraculously
spans the chasm, and the opera concludes with a magnificent
quartet.

The Imperial Couple stand high above the human crowd
among the clouds, while Barak and his Wife are farther down,
more earthbound. But all four of them are united now in sur-
passing and all-embracing happiness.

Intermezzo

$\mathcal{T}$HE YEAR 1924 brought a most pleasant surprise; Strauss, it turned out, wanted me for the premiere of his *Intermezzo* at the Dresden Opera. I do not imagine the good people of Dresden were overenthusiastic at the idea of having the main role go to a guest star rather than to one of their own excellent Staatsoper singers. But Strauss faced them with the choice of having me and a premiere or of having neither. He was determined to have the premiere at Vienna rather than have someone else sing the role.

I was, of course, most happy about this signal expression of artistic confidence on his part and eagerly set out to study the role. The *Sprechgesang* was rather a novelty to me, and the score seemed to present almost insurmountable obstacles. I had always sung roles with swinging cantilenas, and this libretto taken from everyday life gave me no end of trouble. Nowadays, of course, no singer would experience the slightest difficulty with either the music or the words, but at the time they both presented a radical departure from traditional norms which seemed daring, strange, and challenging.

External circumstances, moreover, were most unfavorable to the task at hand. A stubborn case of bronchitis made it impossible for me to sing, and my physician sternly forbade me even to whisper. But the role had to be studied just the same, and I did so under a cruel teacher: Karl Alwin, at that time the husband of Elisabeth Schumann and a most devoted friend of Richard Strauss. I lay in bed running a temperature, but Alwin showed up just the same, had my bed pushed over next to the piano, and played the odd-sounding phrases over and over. And in the end, doctor's orders or not, I invariably would give up trying to resist the natural impulse and start humming the words along with him, to stop only from time to time whenever my husband stuck his anxious, horrified face in the door to urge me to keep absolutely quiet. Alwin, however, was ruthless; the only thing that mattered as far as he was concerned was for me to learn the part. "What good is that going to do," I'd whisper, furious, "if in the end I have no voice left?"

"Let's go over that page once more," would be his only reply.

But I did learn the part. My voice, moreover, recovered undamaged.

Strauss himself was unable to attend the first rehearsals at Dresden, a fact not calculated to allay my apprehension, particularly as he had warned me casually that I was going to be in for trouble. "The local crowd would have much preferred one of their own for Christine," he said. "They're not likely to be overjoyed at seeing you. What you'll have to do is act the Great Prima Donna to scare everybody out of his wits."

I was speechless with fright.

"Prima donna?" I stammered, almost in tears. "That's one role I'll never be able to act. How can you do this to me, *Herr Doktor?* And now, on top of it all, you're not going to be there with me. It's going to be awful, and don't you be surprised if I don't stick it out. I just can't bear the idea of having people intrigue against me and treat me like an enemy."

Strauss seemed sincerely taken aback.

"What do you mean, you can't bear it? That's part of your profession, for heaven's sake. Since when are you such a touch-me-not?"

It became obvious that I could expect no help or sympathy from that quarter, and I took off for Dresden in great fear and trembling.

It turned out to be not nearly so bad as I had anticipated.

Never for a moment did I assume the airs of a prima donna. Quite the contrary, I acted very much myself, and I believe that my Dresden colleagues soon came to realize that I owed my role to no intrigue. The only one not happy with me was Fritz Busch, the excellent conductor, who felt that in the musical sense I had not made the role really my own, and he was absolutely right. I made many mistakes and "swam" through the whole opera, a practice that drove him to despair. Apparently he was only biding his time, waiting for the arrival of Strauss, convinced that the composer would be quite as dissatisfied with my performance as he himself was, and that in the end the role would go to a Dresden singer after all.

He turned out to be wrong.

When Strauss finally did show up at one of the last rehearsals, I took him aside and told him that he had got me into this, and that it was now up to him to stick up for me, come what might. "You know," I reminded him, "that I have a real passion for 'swimming'. Well, I must confess I am 'swimming' through the whole role of Christine . . ."

Strauss laughed uproariously. I used to adore him in moments such as this one, when his eyes mirrored the whole marvelous mirth of his being and when he magnanimously gave absolution for musical sins.

I still can see him leaning on the piano, watching me, while

I cast warning glances in his direction and tried to ignore Busch, who turned to him at my every mistake, apparently expecting an outburst of Olympian wrath.

Strauss let me finish the first scene. Then, addressing all those present, he said with a smile: "Yes, I know that Lehmann likes to 'swim'. But even when she is swimming, I prefer her to other singers."

I could have hugged him, but I well knew how much he disliked displays of affection.

Strauss is supposed initially to have commissioned Hugo von Hofmannsthal to write the libretto for *Intermezzo*, which is based on an episode in his own life, the two main characters representing the composer and his wife, Pauline. It is, in fact, one magnificent declaration of love by the husband to his wife. But when Hofmannsthal brought him the draft of the libretto, Strauss—so legend has it—was horrified because his wife had been turned into a mean and nasty shrew, and on the spot he decided to write the libretto himself. I have no idea whether there is any substance to the story, but *se non è vero è ben trovato*.

Pauline Strauss was incredibly rude on occasion, but fierce in her stubborn integrity. To Strauss, essentially a simple man sick of being constantly surrounded by adulation, her down-to-earth attitude toward him and his success must have offered piquant and refreshing contrast. In *Intermezzo* he certainly presented her in all her many-faceted and ever-contradictory complexity, making a great effort to be objective. In fact, he may on occasion have gone a trifle too far in that direction.

For in the opera the very aspects of her personality which in real life he without a doubt found interesting and attractive emerge as downright unpleasant. Investing the role of Christine with a measure of charm proved to be a difficult task. She is meant to be provocative, and her husband's love and affection for her should always be obvious to the audience. But it is rather tricky to be charming if the libretto requires you to say "Shut your big mouth."

It was truly touching to witness the care that Strauss lavished at rehearsals upon making sure that his Pauline-Christine corresponded in every detail to the personality of his wife. He frequently interrupted with a peremptory: "No, my wife wouldn't do that." And when he said to me "Lotte, you're really so much like my wife in your whole being," I accepted it as the greatest compliment ever paid me. In fact, I had to swallow hard a few times before I could trust myself to thank him.

When all is said and done, what can strangers ever really fathom about the secrets of a heart in love? I had seen much in the Strauss ménage that rather worried me and that seemed incomprehensible; yet Pauline was and remained Strauss's beloved wife. I am utterly convinced that he was deeply happy at her side, and that between them there existed harmony and understanding beyond all appearance, that their marriage served as the fundamental inspiration for many of Strauss's immortal works.

At the Dresden premiere, Strauss proved very eager to have both the stage design and the makeup of Robert Storch as close to their real-life models as possible. Joseph Correck, who sang the role of Conductor Storch, bore a faint resemblance to Strauss which was underscored to the greatest extent possible by makeup. As for myself, however, I in no way resembled the slender, petite Pauline, which may have been a source of disappointment to Strauss. On the other hand, he also may have been convinced right from the start that no one could possibly resemble his Pauline.

Strauss called his *Intermezzo* a "bourgeois comedy with symphonic interludes," a definition that at least hints at the radical innovations that confronted the singers of the period. We were all rather excited during rehearsals, especially as with increasing delight we felt our way into this novel manner of singing. To detail the plot of the comedy presents some difficulties, and I shall limit myself to essentials. The entire beginning was apparently lifted almost verbatim from real life as lived in the Strauss home.

Robert Storch is about to leave on a trip. His wife insists on helping with the suitcases, that is, creating chaos and confusion. An argument flares up between them, with Christine bitterly complaining about household chores, the burden of which rests exclusively on her own frail shoulders. True, they have servants—something which in those days still presented no problem—but servants or no servants, they have to be supervised. Bills have to be paid. Orders have to be written. Errands have to be taken care of. Robert, of course, would not know about things like that, *petit bourgeois* that he is, born and raised in a lower-middle-class home in which the complexities of running a truly refined upper-class home never even could be imagined.

The husband quickly loses his patience and seeks refuge in the dining room.

The chambermaid enters, and the two women now put the finishing touches to the job of packing, which includes an array of medications sufficient to fill a drugstore and to ward off any conceivable illness. Christine complains about her husband being unbearably touchy and quick-tempered; she thinks of herself as cheerful at the prospect of doing without him for a while, but the chambermaid knows better—the instant the master is gone, the lady will start crying and feeling lonesome. Would she perhaps like to go sleigh riding in this wonderful winter weather?

Robert returns, more laconic than ever, and his manners once again provoke a fight. Christine simply cannot, or rather does not want to understand the artist's temperament. To translate one's most private emotions into music and thus reveal them to a vulgar crowd of curiosity seekers strikes her as downright obscene, and she, at any rate, will never have her name bandied about by an indifferent or hostile public, be it contemporary or future.

Poor Pauline. That was unquestionably one of her own remarks. In this opera Strauss certainly erected a monument to her.

Christine attempts to make the parting between her husband and herself as tempestuous as possible. That is to say, a tempestuous quarrel is the guiding melody in this scene. Robert leaves the house in a fit of indignation, but in his heart of hearts he means it no more than his wife does; the two are well matched in mutual misunderstanding.

And now that her husband is gone, the chambermaid will have to serve as scapegoat for Christine. Lisl von Schuch sang the role of the chambermaid in Dresden and was both delightful and convincing.

Intermezzo requires many very quick changes of costume. I wore a different dress in every scene, and the breaks between them were so short that I was always out of breath when I reappeared. From negligee into a winter outfit within seconds, and it still seems inconceivable that it should always have come off without a hitch.

The second scene required my sledding down a "snow-covered" hill, the ride ending in a head-on collision with the young Baron Lummer, who comes skiing down the same hill from the other side. The blame, of course, is all Christine's— she simply has been paying no attention to where she is going —but this does not stop her from waxing indignant at the young fellow. "You silly ass," she splutters, "can't you see that people are coming down the hill?" She calms down rather quickly, however, upon discovering that the Baron happens to be the son of a colonel with whom she is well acquainted.

Pauline Strauss herself came from a well-known officers'

family and displayed a lifelong weakness for things and persons military. Strauss took great pains to describe the real-life situation, and on the stage Christine therefore turns out to be charmed instantly by the dashing young gentleman, delighted to discover that they both belong to the same "class" of people. She immediately extends an invitation, which is accepted with alacrity and manifest pleasure.

From winter clothes into a dirndl, and then the curtain rises upon Christine and the Baron as they laughingly descend the staircase of the Grundlseewirt Inn, where they have been dancing until even Christine has had her fill. She is happy and all aglow with pure pleasure. The Baron, on the other hand, seems somewhat embarrassed by her forthright manner of asking him when in heaven's name he is going to settle down and start studying in earnest. Personally, as it happens, he much prefers dancing to studying, which at the moment does not bother Christine one bit. Robert cannot dance and always begs off on the pretext that it makes him dizzy. Christine is so very fond of dancing, and the Baron is only too happy to oblige. Once again they get out on the dance floor.

From dirndl into fur coat and fur cap, with split-second timing. Christine descends upon the Notary's wife from whom the Baron has rented a room. Yes, she had promised to make sure that he would get a decent room, and now she imparts the story of the Baron's life, informing that compassionate lady that her new tenant is suffering from the most devasting migraines, poor fellow, which unfortunately prevent him from attending regular classes at the university. A congenital disease, so it seems. But the altitude here is most helpful in cases such as his, though what he needs is a comfortable armchair. Aside, of course, from absolute, scrupulous, antiseptic around-the-clock cleanliness—which, as she can tell from just a glance, is not really being observed at the Notary's house, though the good lady may delude herself into thinking it is. The closets, for instance, will have to be thoroughly washed both inside and out. Christine's own maid will take care of that. And thus, with a regal nod, she takes her leave, seen to the door by a now thoroughly rattled housewife.

Another split-second change, leaving us limp with fear.

Christine, in a pretty housedress, sitting at her desk. She has just finished a letter to her husband and rereads it with all the pleasure of an artist having just accomplished a great work of art. She is particularly pleased by the masterful parting phrase, "Your poor, neglected wife." Just let him put that in his pipe and smoke it; what does he expect her to do, anyway —mope around here waiting for him to come back? He will just have to accept the fact that the Baron has become a good friend with whom she can go for walks, dance, or engage in winter sports, all of them distractions that Robert loathes.

Christine is pleased that, for once, someone is coming to the house for her sake rather than for that of her famous husband. Everyone she knows is all but dying with awe and reverence for Robert. To hell with them all. She hates all this pretentiousness and longs for the simple joys of middle-class life.

The cook interrupts her rebellious deliberations and wants her to check the accounts.

Bookkeeping, of course, happens to be a thoroughly domestic occupation, but once again Christine just does not feel like doing it. She wants to be left alone; and as for the menu, she does not care what is being served.

Baron Lummer arrives. He offers to help with the bills, but appears distracted, absentminded, eager to say something, but at the same time afraid to come out with it. Christine is no help, either; every time he opens his mouth, she interrupts him; besides, she has not yet had a chance to read today's newspaper, and finds this just the appropriate moment. Magnanimously she offers to share part of the paper with him.

The whole scene is extraordinarily funny. What the Baron

really wants is to ask for a loan of a thousand marks. After all, she has been so very kind to him, and what does he have to lose? But whenever he screws up his courage, she interrupts and starts on something else. She keeps talking about her husband, praising him to the skies—a great man, and a most generous one, who will certainly help the Baron in every way possible. The Baron finally gives up and takes his leave without ever having had the nerve to bring up his request. They make a date for the following day, and Christine watches him leave with an almost tender expression on her face. What a handsome young man. But that is all she sees in him. As to her husband, oh, she wishes he were back already; she feels so lonesome without him.

A beautiful flowing tune expresses her thoughts, the first time that Christine's spirit is rendered by harmony. Might that not have been the sort of tune Strauss cherished for her in his own heart?

Next scene: The Baron's room.

The Baron is rather at odds with the world and himself today. He is debating whether or not to make an overt declaration of love, but how can he be sure that Christine would be receptive? In all likelihood, she would respond by singing the praise of her great and beloved husband. This business of reading newspapers à deux definitely is not his cup of tea. He finally decides to ask for the loan by letter. Migraines indeed —that woman would believe anything.

And, laughing out loud, he starts writing.

In a rapid switch we are taken back to Christine's room, where she stands, holding a letter, struck dumb with fury. So that is what he was after, all along. Money. What an impertinence. And for once she had thought that someone came for her sake alone, with no hidden designs! It had done her good to feel that someone was interested in her rather than in her famous husband. And now this! Out of the question.

The Baron, hopeful, appears in the door, but is made to step back, first of all, and wipe his feet, what with all that snow outside. Next, Christine curtly informs him that he is deluding himself if he thinks that she will lend him money. Moreover, if he really needs a thousand marks, why not go out and earn them? He could give lessons, for instance.

Lessons? He starts up in horror. Lessons, in addition to his strenuous and exhausting studies? And his delicate health? Utterly impossible. Preposterous.

In the midst of this rather painful confrontation, a letter is delivered, addressed to Christine's husband. Thinking that she recognizes the handwriting, Christine opens the envelope and immediately utters a cry of stark horror, staring at the paper in her hand. Written by someone named Mieze Meier, who addresses her very own husband as "My darling," the note requests two tickets to the opera; Mieze will meet him in the bar later on "as always."

Christine here turns openly histrionic, and the dramatic outcry with which she announces her fainting spell is irresistibly funny because it is obvious at once that the letter could not possibly have been addressed to Robert and that the whole thing must be based on a misunderstanding.

Christine alone is convinced of the opposite. As she sees it, Robert has been unmasked at long last. She knew it, of course; she suspected it all along. But here is proof positive. This is the end.

The Baron is only too happy to beat a hasty retreat while Christine in trembling haste pens the following telegram: "You know Mieze Meier. Have proof you deceived me. Don't ever want to see you again."

Summoning the maid, she orders all her things packed immediately. She is leaving at once and forever.

This scene would have been a rather effective conclusion to the act, but unfortunately Strauss found it necessary to add another, so full of cloying sentimentality that I always have found it downright embarrassing.

Christine is seated on the edge of little Franz's bed, telling her son about his bad daddy and how Franz and she ought to go away and leave him. Franz starts to cry, rebelling desperately. His daddy, he sobs, is a good man, and it is his mother who always acts mean and picks fights. Christine, of course, protests. She has put up with that father of his altogether too long, much longer than he deserved, and this is going to be the end. From now on Franz will be a poor fatherless little boy, and she herself will be a poor abandoned wife. Prayerfully, she kneels by the bedside.

Strauss was obviously taken aback when I told him that I rather disliked this ending. He objected that his wife would have acted in just this manner, and as Christine was supposed to be identical with Pauline, that was the way it had to be.

Well, who am I to argue with the great Richard Strauss about his work?

The applause following the first-act curtain in both Dresden and Vienna was such that I may well be wrong.

Strauss loved to play skat. The game to him was hobby and relaxation, and wherever he found three partners willing to play, they became his pals—at least for the duration of that evening. And the task of describing the game in a musical setting must have been pure pleasure to him. He does it at the beginning of the second act of *Intermezzo*, and I still remember how absolutely radiant he seemed at rehearsals, almost as though wanting to sit down right then and there at the table and transform the musical game into a real one. Sometime ago I met his son, Dr. Franz Strauss; and when I told him about this book, then still in the planning stage, he warned me not to write too much about his father's passion for skat. "Everybody," he said, "writes about my father as though all his life he hadn't done a thing other than play skat."

What a strange idea!

As the curtain rises, four men are grouped around a table. They are the Counselor-at-Law, the Commercial Counselor, the Royal Chamber Singer, and the conductor named Stroh. Robert has not yet arrived, and the other four talk about him with open admiration, at the same time displaying considerably less affection for his wife. The Commercial Counselor in particular waxes rather eloquent about his dislike of Christine. "Do you know her?" he asks the Counselor-at-Law. "A harridan. He is a delightful fellow; but as for her—horrible is the word."

These remarks are all dropped by the way, as it were, quite incidental to the main business of playing the game. At last Robert, delayed by rehearsals, arrives to join his friends, and here we have Strauss's own confession, put in the mouth of Robert Storch, his alter ego in the opera: "Nothing like a game of skat, the only relaxation after music."

The game continues. The Counselor-at-Law, however, cannot help himself when something urges him to bring the conversation around to the despicable Christine once again. Robert immediately responds to the attack, and the hymn he sings in praise of his beloved wife is one of the most touching accolades Strauss ever bestowed upon his Pauline. He sees her as a temperamental girl with a lively imagination, touchingly helpless and childish. "She is just exactly right for me," he exclaims. "I tend to let myself go in daydreams and indolence. Whatever I have accomplished I owe to her alone, especially my health. I need her. I need life and excitement around me. Everyone has more than one facet to him, but most people show only their pleasant side, whereas she is different. She is a jewel in a rough setting."

An instant later he holds a telegram just delivered and in horrified bewilderment reads the contents. "You know Mieze Meier. . . ."

Mieze Meier? Robert never even has heard the name, but his partners all smack their lips at the mere mention; they never would have thought that a solid citizen like Robert had anything to do with the likes of Mieze Meier. Hmmm . . . Knowing the lady as well as they do, the gentlemen are about to leer when Robert precipitately leaves the room, rushing out like a madman. His excitement is understandable; confronting Christine even without any particular issues at stake always is somewhat like walking into a lion's cage. In the circumstances, the best one can hope for is that for Robert's sake the affair will be settled in some more or less satisfactory manner. Whereupon the gentlemen go on with their game.

The Lawyer's study. Christine enters, huffing with pomp and dignity. She wants to get a divorce. The first thing that occurs to the Lawyer, of course, is the young Baron, but Christine indignantly explains that on the contrary it is Robert who has committed adultery and from whom she wants a divorce. And the terms of the settlement are clear: everything is to go to her—the house, the child, liquid assets, everything.

The Lawyer is somewhat overwhelmed and asks to see her evidence. She hands him the letter signed Mieze Meier, and, upon reading it carefully, he ventures to point out that this may, after all, turn out to have been a simple mistake of some sort, a misunderstanding. Christine will not hear of it; all she wants to know is whether or not he is willing to start divorce proceedings on her behalf. When he insists that he would first want to talk to her husband, she storms out of the room, sarcastically pointing out that other lawyers perhaps will be more inclined to serve their clients' needs.

1916: As the Composer
in *Ariadne auf Naxos*.
This was the role that catapulted
Lotte Lehmann to fame.

schiedel-Setzer, Vienna)

1919: As the Dyer's Wife
in *Die Frau ohne Schatten*.
Maria Jeritza claimed that Strauss
offered her the role first
but changed his mind and gave
her the part of the Empress.

(Ellinger, Salzburg)

)24: As Christine in *Intermezzo*.
his role was closely patterned after Strauss's wife, Pauline.
lfred Jerger sang opposite Madame Lehmann.

1933: In the title role
of *Arabella*.
Lotte Lehmann sang
at the Vienna premiere
under the most difficult
circumstances—
her mother had died
a few hours before
curtain time.

Der Rosenkavalier: Lotte Lehmann
is the only great star
to have played all three leading soprano
roles in this opera.
First, Sophie (left),
then Octavian (below),
and then, in 1924, for the first time
the Marschallin (right).
This became the role for which
she was perhaps most famous.

(*Letzer, Vienna*)

(Carlo Edwards, New York)

Madame Lehmann herself painted
this portrait of the great composer
with whom she was so closely associated
for so many years.

Richard Strauss gave this photo of himself
to Madame Lehmann in 1947.
His inscription on it reads:
"To the unforgettable Lotte . . ."

1957: Madame Lehmann in her studio at Santa Barbara, California.

In the meantime, Robert has been sending wire after wire to his wife, asserting total and unequivocal innocence. Not a single one has been answered. He is completely beside himself, the more so because the terms of his contract force him to stay on as conductor throughout the festival, so that he cannot follow his impulse to rush home.

In the next scene we find him walking in the Prater, the beautiful park in the surroundings of Vienna; and here the conductor Stroh, who had been looking for him everywhere, finally manages to track him down. Stroh, it turns out, is suffering from an acute case of bad conscience; he dimly suspects that he himself unwittingly unleashed this whole domestic drama, which of course does not lack humorous aspects to all but those involved. Stroh, at any rate, fails to see the humor of the situation, and tremblingly explains that unquestionably Mieze Meier had mistaken *him*, the insignificant little conductor Stroh, for the famous conductor *Storch;* the point that he had taken no great pains to disabuse her of this notion naturally needs not to be labored. In any event she now apparently has looked up Storch's address in the directory and sent the fatal letter.

Robert, outraged at the ridiculous pretensions of this bandleader, is ready to murder the man; he gives him orders to take himself to Grundlsee forthwith, see Christine, and clear up this mess at once. The culprit, crushed, agrees to do as told.

High time, at that; for Christine has in the meantime packed everything and emptied the house of whatever was not bolted down. The room is in an indescribable state of chaos, with Christine racing back and forth, issuing a constant stream of contradictory orders that threaten to drive the maid Anna to the verge of insanity. Christine has dispatched the Baron to Vienna with orders to interrogate Mieze Meier; the evidence in her hands is obviously not altogether convincing, and what she wants is Mieze Meier's own admission. Unfortunately, the

Baron failed to take with him a picture of her husband which would permit positive identification. But Christine feels that in the end her husband himself can go to see that woman if he really is as innocent as he makes himself out to be in the telegrams that keep arriving at all hours of the day and night and which she has stopped reading altogether. Yet a slight shadow of doubt has begun to mar the pristine purity of her indignation.

Another wire arrives, and this time at Anna's insistence Christine reads the contents and begins to suspect some of the real causes underlying the confusion.

"Unfortunate error," she reads. "Name confused with that of colleague Stroh, who will arrive tomorrow to prove facts to you in person. Your innocent and most happy Robert."

At this point Stroh is being announced, and the curtain drops before the audience can be present at the meeting.

In the next scene we at first see Christine happy and excited; her husband is coming home at last, and all the quarrels and recriminations will be laid to rest.

But the moment he enters, radiant, ready to forgive and forget, she immediately reins in her feelings, loath to admit her error and acknowledge her happiness. Once more the "rough shell" that Robert had described so aptly and movingly to his friends closes in and traps her loving heart. Feigning incredulity, she arches her eyebrows. "I suppose," she remarks haughtily, "that you assume everything is now in the best of order, don't you?"

Here I should like to digress briefly with an account of an incident that, though embarrassing when it happened, seems rather hilarious in retrospect. Once in the course of all those countless performances of *Intermezzo*, the inevitable finally happened—the change of costume did not quite succeed.

When the lights came on, I discovered that I had slipped back-side forward into my charming negligee, with the back constricting me in front and the front flapping down loosely in the back. It was a rather obvious predicament, and when, with customary hauteur, I asked my stage husband Alfred Jerger—a first-rate Robert Storch—if "he assumed that everything was now in the best of order," he was seized by so irresistible an urge to laugh that for several seconds neither of us could quite manage to go on. However, I do not think the audience noticed, as we rallied quickly and went on bickering in the style of the opera.

But now it is Robert's turn to get angry. He is so clearly in the right and has for so long been putting up with his wife's irrational fits that for once all his accumulated anger explodes in one mighty eruption. The music picks up with powerful chords, and his "I've had enough of this nonsense" makes for a breathtaking and dramatically forceful exit. Christine stands there, crestfallen and petrified, seeing her worst fears confirmed. But before she even has time to feel properly sorry for herself, the Baron enters to report on his trip to Vienna and his futile interview with Mieze Meier. She was no help because he did not have a picture of the maestro. Christine, treating him with the utmost condescension, wants to know why he did not go out and buy one; they were available in any bookstore, after all. She is being rather nasty to the poor little Baron, whose usefulness has ended as far as she is concerned, and she insists on making it quite plain that she never for one moment doubted her husband's devotion. She had known right from the start that it was all a stupid mistake.

The Baron exits, shaking his head, unable to make head or tail of this bizarre behavior.

Robert returns. He has calmed down and is ready once again for a reconciliation. Christine, in turn, is being very sweet and gentle, realizing for once that she has been in the wrong. Moreover, she was greatly impressed by his outburst; his shouting her down has somehow proved him to be a man after all. She mentions the Baron, and Robert teases her gently about her blueblooded admirer, but when he finds out that the Baron wanted to borrow money, he cannot help laughing. Poor little Christine; he so well understands what a letdown that must have been. And he declares himself ready to help the Baron if for no other reason than gratitude for the Baron's kindness during his own absence. Furthermore, he suspects that with him Christine never quarreled—a fact Christine is quick to affirm. The Baron, she admits, was much too weak and wishy-washy to make fighting worth her while. On the other hand, where did Robert get the idea that she always would swallow her pride and let him be in the right?

And now the music that Strauss had heretofore largely saved for the interludes breaks out in a broad stream, reflecting the essential harmony of these two human beings and buoying them up as on a torrent of ineffable beauty.

Christine promises that she never again will contradict her husband, avowing that only when she saw him towering above her in his wrath did she really understand what he was like. How tall, how beautiful he looked in his anger! "You are my beautiful, my pure, my only beloved husband, and I shall love you, and you alone, forever and ever."

And he, in turn, forgives her. He would forgive her anything for the sake of this one transcendent moment of life-giving truth. And as they embrace, Christine says to her beloved husband: "Ours is a truly happy marriage, isn't it, Robert?"

This then, was Richard Strauss's confession and testament, proof that he was happy at the side of the often misunderstood Pauline, her true being known to him alone.

I should have known better than to make a careless remark in Pauline's presence when, after the first performance, we crowded into the hotel elevator, surrounded by a mass of people who all had been to the opera and were now ogling Pauline and her famous husband with undisguised curiosity. "This opera," I said, "is really a marvelous present to you from your husband, isn't it?"

Tensely everybody waited for her answer. She looked around, cast a quick glance at her husband, then said in a loud, clear voice: "I don't give a damn."

Embarrassed silence.

Strauss smiled.

Arabella

SOME TIME AGO, as I sat in a beautiful patio garden in
Pasadena, a gentleman came up to introduce himself and, with
due apologies, inquired how it came about that I had not
sung at the premiere of *Arabella*.

My answer, I'm afraid, must have struck him as rather un-
satisfactory, if indeed he believed me in the first place. The
simple truth is that I have forgotten the reason. Quite possibly
I was in the United States at the time of the Dresden premiere,
or—and more likely—Strauss preferred the younger Viorica
Ursuleac, an excellent singer. I do not recall whether at the
time she already was married to Clemens Krauss, but in any
case she was on close terms with him, and Krauss in turn
happened to be a fanatical admirer of Strauss as well as his
sincerely devoted friend. It therefore seems likely that Strauss
preferred Viorica Ursuleac for the role.

I did, however, sing at the Vienna premiere in October,
1933, and under the most trying circumstances conceivable:
my beloved mother had died on the eve of the premiere.

Krauss, our manager, called at once to say that everyone

understood what this death meant to me and that therefore he scarcely dared to ask if I would consider going on just the same. However, I should bear in mind that critics from all over had come to Vienna especially for this performance, that of course it had been sold out long before and that—as there could be no possible substitution for a Strauss premiere—the house for the first time in history would have to be closed if I refused. Viorica Ursuleac was due to sing Arabella that same night in Berlin and therefore could not take my place.

Crushed as I was by the burden of my loss, by the death of what to me was the best mother in the world, I could react only with a lethargic assent: "I'll go on."

It was an experience I shall never forget. No power in the world is greater than that of music. For two brief hours it enabled me to forget my deep personal grief, to be Arabella rather than my own tormented, pain-racked, and mourning self. This, in my opinion, is the highest kind of satisfaction our work has to offer, the magic ability to transform and transcend one's self, to escape from the gray routine of everyday life into a different and far more fascinating world. Blessed work, after all; and how grateful I was for that premiere.

Strauss, profoundly touched by my consent to go ahead and sing, wanted to take me out with him to the footlights at the end of the performance, but I had to refuse. I had done all I could, but I certainly did not want to be applauded for having, by the grace of God, passed a test.

Thus Strauss himself stepped out instead and announced that he would accept the thanks of the audience on behalf of Lotte Lehmann.

Toscanini attended this performance and heard me for the first time. Later on he told me how very moved he had been.

The crowd waiting at the stage door for the artist after the show usually is a rather noisy and unruly group, and it was especially so after a Strauss premiere. My nerves that night were stretched taut, ready to snap, and I dreaded having to face them. But for once I had done the Viennese a grave injustice by underestimating their tact. To a man they felt with me and for me, standing by in absolute silence, hats off, as I passed, in one of the most moving tributes I ever have received, giving me proof of their love and respect. There was no way for me to repay their kindness, but I often have thanked them in my heart, and I do so once again.

The strength to sing, to do one's duty in extremes of adversity, to defy personal despair is an artist's most blessed gift. There is, there can be, no such excuse as "I cannot do it." I have sung lengthy roles while running a high temperature and once I had to finish half an opera with a sprained ankle. I did collapse at the end—but after the performance. *The show must go on* is still the first commandment in show business, and whoever does not have the strength of will and character to live up to it had better choose a different career right from the start.

Outsiders get to see only the so-called glamour surrounding artists and never suspect the extremes of self-denial, disappointment, and constant inner struggle which comprise the very fundamental aspects of our profession. But however great its sacrifices, the rewards are splendid indeed.

Nothing equals the grandeur and detachment of artistic creation, and the Vienna *Arabella* premiere of October 21, 1933, proved this to me once again.

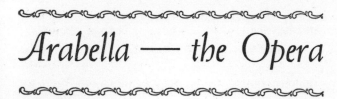

Arabella — the Opera

COUNT WALDNER has gambled away his family's fortune, his home, his estate and moved to Vienna with his wife and two daughters. He has chosen a first-class hotel, as befits his status, but for some time now has been remiss in paying his rent and all his other bills. Consequently he is now faced with the embarrassing predicament of having all his credit cut off and being forced to pay cash for whatever he wants. But he still holds one trump card—his older daughter, Arabella, a great beauty: if he can find a wealthy suitor for her, his troubles are over. This scheme, of course, requires a proper debut among the Viennese aristocracy, and the expense already is far beyond his means; it would manifestly be impossible to repeat this sort of performance, and therefore the younger daughter, Zdenka, must be passed off as a boy until Arabella's marriage has successfully repaired the damage to the family fortune. Zdenka always has been a tomboy, anyway, and has played her role in Vienna with exquisite skill. Then an unforeseen complication arises in the shape of dashing young Lieutenant Matteo, Arabella's ardent suitor. Zdenka has fallen in love with him, while he, in turn, sees in her only his friend "Zdenko," the kid brother of his beloved Arabella. The poor girl has no hope of marrying Matteo, but she loves him from the bottom of her heart and, in a wholly unselfish and self-sacrificing manner, wants him to be happy. And because his happiness seems to depend on his possessing Arabella, Zdenka begs her older sister to grant Matteo her favors.

Arabella, however, is determined to go her own way and to steer clear of marriage intrigues. She is not in love with any of the young men who are drawn to her like moths to a flame, and she has no intention whatever of giving herself to any of them. In fact, she does not intend to get married— not just yet, much to the despair of her mercenary parents, who, though not hostile to the impecunious Matteo, definitely are counting on a wealthy match for Arabella, preferably marriage to the millionaire Count Elemer.

Queenlike, Arabella divides her favor impartially among three suitors, preferring none, wanting none, concealing her true thoughts and feelings. She moves among men as a stranger, cool and aloof. One word from her could take her family from rags to riches, but she will not utter it.

As the curtain rises, her mother, a woman living in a fairy-tale world of her own, is about to consult a soothsayer, an old hag who prattles about a wealthy suitor for Arabella. This obviously means Count Elemer. The question is whether her daughter finally will accept him. Will she finally come around and understand that filial duty requires her to help her family? The poor mother, torn between dark prophecies and promising possibilities, gives herself over to delicious daydreams while Zdenka tries to cope with the creditors presenting unpaid bills. If only Arabella would accept Count Elemer . . . If all turns out well, the soothsayer will be given the precious brooch, the last piece of jewelry not yet pawned. By a few cunning questions, the old hag elicits the secret of Zdenka's true sex and thereupon informs the mother that the cards clearly indicate complications, notably a duel. A woman is trying to come between the wealthy suitor and the older daughter.

Countess Waldner, unable to bear the suspense any longer, drags the soothsayer into an adjacent room for still another go at the cards, just to discover if fate does not, after all, hold some great good fortune for them.

Zdenka, alone, is in open despair. What if the cards prove right and Arabella does marry Count Elemer? Matteo may well kill himself; after all, he loves Arabella more than anything, more than his life. What could she possibly do to help him? Secretly, with her handwriting disguised to resemble that of her sister, she already has written him a number of epistles—passionate love letters supposedly signed by Arabella, just so he could be happy for an hour or two. But how long can this go on? One of these days he is bound to find out what happened, and the prospect of an ultimate confrontation looms over Zdenka like a nightmare.

Matteo himself appears and interrupts her musings. He wants to know where Arabella is and whether Zdenko by any chance has a letter for him. Zdenko must help him once again, must urge Arabella to yield to him because he simply can no longer live without her. If she refuses, if once again she proves hard-hearted, he will take his pistol and shoot himself. That's the only way out.

With this threat he leaves.

Poor Zdenka. She is supposed to help him, but she herself has no one to turn to.

Arabella is coming home from a walk which, consonant with her social status, she took in the company of a chaperone. She seems strangely excited and, seeing the roses on the table, wants to know right away if by any chance a hussar brought them.

It turns out that she has had a curious experience. In the street she met a stranger whose dark eyes captivated her at once so that she, the proud and distant one, for the first time in her life felt her heart beat faster for a man. The stranger's image remained etched on her memory and in her very soul. When Zdenka mentions Matteo, Arabella merely shrugs her shoulders, profoundly wounding her younger sister. No one, Zdenka feels, is worthier of Arabella's love; she herself can only hope and pray that fate will preserve her from becoming as cold and hardhearted as her beautiful sister.

Arabella turns to Zdenka with a very grave mien, disclosing for the first time the true secret of her innermost being. Yes, she knows herself to be fickle and frivolous; she easily falls in and out of love with a man. As for Matteo, she once rather liked him—very briefly. A caprice long since forgotten. But one day *he* will come, *he* for whom she has been waiting patiently all these years. She'll know him the moment she lays eyes on him, and she will give herself to him, to the right one, to be his forever, his obedient and devoted slave.

Zdenka listens in astonishment, for this is the first time Arabella has opened her heart to her. The bitterness between them changes into gentle sympathy. For once Zdenka fails to mention Matteo; she wants her sister to be happy at the side of the right man.

The duet between the two women is one of the most beautiful things in this opera, winged melodies blending the two soprano voices in one delightful harmony.

Count Elemer's sleigh has arrived, and Zdenka is greatly worried about the dashing Count's finding favor in Arabella's eyes. Arabella seems to be vacillating. Today is Mardi Gras; tomorrow life begins in earnest, and perhaps she ought to accept a suitor as wealthy as Count Elemer. Zdenka, on the other hand, can think only of Matteo's reaction; the poor boy is likely to kill himself. She takes the red roses from the vase and presses them to Arabella's bosom: only he who sent these roses is worthy of her.

Count Elemer's arrival interrupts the emotional scene, and Zdenka withdraws.

Elemer, buoyant and full of verve, informs Arabella of a bet among her three suitors. Arabella is to choose one of them this very day. As for himself, his horses are waiting outside, ready to whisk their beautiful mistress with lightning speed through the avenues of the Prater.

Elemer's resolute directness shakes Arabella's detachment for an instant. She agrees to go with him, sit in the sleigh with him, and go storming through the park—provided, however, that Zdenka comes along. The Count is crestfallen. He desperately had wanted to be alone with her, and declare his love in a passionate speech. And now the brat is to come along and wreck his plans. Well, he'll have to accept, being given no choice.

Arabella dismisses him with a conciliatory, "See you soon."

She has been charming with him throughout this scene, behavior that presents the actress portraying her with a number of dangerous pitfalls. For one thing, she must never actually flirt with Count Elemer, must not stoop to his level, as it were. Rather, she must depict the aloof amiability of a *grande dame* graciously granting a favor. Arabella's outstanding characteristic is her invincible pride, and she remains far too remote and unattainable to her suitors to do more than offer her hand condescendingly for them to kiss. Only one, and he alone, will tame this pride and transmute it into humble devotion— the man for whom she has been waiting.

Zdenka returns. She is reluctant to go along on the sleigh ride with Count Elemer, whom she does not like. In order to cheer her up, Arabella wants to show her the beautiful horses waiting outside, but she recoils from the window with an outcry. She has seen the Stranger; he is standing outside. If

Zdenka but knew what a shock it was to see him. And once again Arabella's cold proud heart is beating madly; she must tell her sister, she must talk to someone about it. But their parents' precipitate arrival interrupts the sisters' intimacy. Count Waldner is profoundly depressed, and the Countess, suspecting the worst, sends "the children" out of the room in order to have a few moments alone with him—time enough to confirm her worst fears. Once again the Count has gambled and lost. This is their fate, their accursed fate which could be changed into good fortune by one word from Arabella.

Count Waldner thereupon tells his wife a rather strange story. There used to be a regimental comrade of his, a wealthy officer by the name of Mandryka. Delightful fellow, good sport, but out-and-out crazy. Once, in the middle of August, he had the streets of Verona covered with salt just because a pretty girl felt like going for a sleigh ride. If that man so much as caught a glimpse of Arabella . . . Well, as a matter of fact he, Count Waldner, recently had written to him and enclosed a picture of Arabella, just on an impulse. Mandryka might like the picture, and then—there is no telling what might happen.

The Countess is indignant at the thought of having Arabella married off to an old man, but Count Waldner sees no other way out. With all these young and handsome suitors around, what does Arabella do? Flirt, tease, mock, play as though she had all the time in the world instead of being haunted by ruin. This must stop. There is no other possibility.

The Countess, meanwhile, has been thinking and, as always, has drifted off into rosy dreams of her own. There is Aunt Ludwiga, rich old Aunt Ludwiga . . . They'll move into her castle, and everything will turn out all right. Arabella will make a splendid match because the soothsayer practically has guaranteed that she will. Furthermore, she herself dreamed no less than three lucky numbers, so everything is bound to come out all right.

The Count has heard these fairy tales often enough to be sick of them and knows exactly what he can expect of that famous Aunt Ludwiga of hers. Selling the emerald brooch is a far surer way of getting much-needed money; the brooch is the very last piece of a small treasure in jewels that gradually has been pawned. Now the Countess is greatly embarrassed in turn: she already has used the brooch to pay the soothsayer, but after all, that was one way of making certain that her prophecies will come true. The last heirloom, then, is gone, and the family faces the abyss of ultimate ruin.

Vienna did it. Vienna is to blame—lighthearted, beautiful, irresponsible Vienna.

Arabella, however, will rise victorious out of this misery and be happy. Love matches happen even in royal families. The Countess is very firm about this, and leaves on this note of assurance.

Her husband scarcely has been listening, having been busy with his own calculations. For one thing, he very badly needs a glass of cognac, but the waiter will not let him have one on credit. Furthermore, he is terribly upset because he knows that at this moment he'd be bound to win, if he only had a little bit of money to get him started again in the game. As it is, he does not have a penny to his name, and no one in the world will give him credit.

The waiter knocks to announce a visitor.

Another creditor, no doubt, come to hound him.

But a second later Waldner does a double take. What is this, a creditor sending up his card? He looks at it and, seeing the name Mandryka, can scarcely contain his delight. At last!

My old army buddy . . . With wide open arms, Count Waldner rushes forward to meet his friend and finds himself abruptly face to face with a total stranger.

Old Mandryka, it quickly develops, has passed away, and Count Waldner is about to meet the old man's nephew and heir.

Here I cannot help mentioning Alfred Jerger, my Mandryka in Vienna. It was a magnificent role for this many-faceted actor, a singing actor in the true, full sense of those words. He imparted a special flavor to each of his roles, and his Mandryka was a man of a very special cast—gentleman and country squire, honest, ingenuous, generous, but awesome and menacing in his wrath.

Another young Mandryka pleased me equally well. In my Arabella performance at the Music Academy of the West, at Santa Barbara, the role was sung by a young singing actor, named Ronald Holgate, whose future holds great promise indeed. He grasped the essence of this complex role to an extent that seemed almost incredible, and it was truly an experience to watch his Mandryka, so different from that of the wise and urbane Jerger, a Mandryka born out of a turbulent temper, savage as a tempest unspent.

I hope that the future will fulfill the promise contained in Ronald Holgate's gifts.

The footman accompanying Mandryka halts at the door. There is an aura of exotic glamour about the master. His tall figure is commanding, and even the diffident, almost shy manner in which he greets Count Waldner barely conceals the fundamental self-assurance of a man accustomed to giving orders.

He divulges his story only upon having made certain first that Arabella is indeed the Count's daughter, and that she is still neither married nor betrothed.

Among his uncle's papers, he explains, he found the picture of Arabella and instantly fell in love with it. He would have rushed to Vienna at once to make her acquaintance, but unfortunately he sustained a very serious injury in the course of a bear hunt, which forced him to spend many weeks recuperating. During that period the incomparable picture came to occupy an ever more important place in his heart.

What he would like to know, among other things, is why the Count enclosed this photograph in a letter to his old regimental comrade.

The Count is a bit hard put to explain his action, but he almost never runs out of excuses. He wanted, he says, to give his old friend some fun.

Mandryka is indignant. Some fun, indeed. His uncle was the male animal through and through, all the way to the end; if he had seen this picture and wanted to possess the girl—what then?

Once again the Count is ready with the answer. "In that case," he says, "I would have found myself in an unexpected predicament."

Mandryka, however, fed up with these hints and innuendoes, is determined to head directly for the point at issue. What he wants is the Count's permission to ask for Arabella's hand. The Count is dumb struck, unable for once even to open his mouth. But Mandryka reads the hoped-for consent in his eyes. And now, with a naïve pride (which *must* be utterly devoid of bragging), he gives an account of his enormous wealth so impressive that even the Count is awed into absolute silence during the recital. All this, to him, is a fairy tale, salvation and redemption at the very last minute. Arabella's hand will change the family's fate from one instant to the next; and how could she possibly refuse this man, so overwhelming, so out-and-out divine? The Count knows his daughter well enough to realize that this time there will be no hesitation and no refusal.

Mandryka shows the Count his wallet, filled with gold. This gold, he explains, once was one of his forests, which he sold in order to have enough cash for this Viennese adventure.

Fascinated, the Count stares at the bulging wallet. Never in his life has he seen that much money. Mandryka gallantly holds out the wallet and urges the Count to help himself. "Go ahead," he says, as though offering a trifling loan.

Count Waldner is quick to seize the opportunity; with a lucky break in his gambling, he could probably double this small fortune in no time. He therefore accepts with pleasure and a great show of dignity, emphasizing that he considers this strictly a loan; he will repay it for sure, now that his luck has changed and he is bound to win.

After Mandryka's departure, the Count is seized by a fit of ecstatic exultation. The words "Please, sir, help yourself" become one refrain of a skipping tune so that Zdenka, rushing in with no idea of what just has occurred, is led to believe that her father, who is skipping around, singing and juggling coins, at long last has lost his mind altogether.

Still singing, the Count walks out on his puzzled and exasperated daughter. A moment later Arabella enters, urging haste; Elemer is waiting and Zdenka has not yet changed. But Zdenka flies into a rage and absolutely refuses to have anything further to do with the whole matter. "To hell with your horses and your Elemer," she cries, indignant, leaving the room.

The words "your Elemer" pierce Arabella's heart like a dagger. Her Elemer? Does he belong to her? Does she belong to him? The idea of belonging to Elemer is akin to the thought of entering her own chill tomb. Never—never of her own free will! She'll not be his, nor Matteo's, either. Once again the image of the Stranger rises before her mind's eye; if only she could speak to him once, hear his voice. Well, what then? What if he should turn out to be like all the others? All those who fleetingly pleased her and whom she forgot just as quickly? Would it be the same story all over again? She banishes those futile thoughts. Useless self-lacerations. He might very well be married, for instance, and in any case she is not likely ever to see him again.

Do not look that far ahead, she admonishes herself. Surrender to the moment. And the moment, right now, means the ball that is to take place tonight, where she will reign as queen. A whirling waltz catches her fancy and sweeps her away, light and supple as though no pain or struggle ever had touched her life.

This waltz concludes Act One.

Arabella and Zdenka leave the room together to meet Count Elemer.

Act Two

The second act depicts the annual *Fiakerball*, a carnival highlight during which all social barriers and distinctions temporarily are abolished, where countess and hack driver, housemaid and baron for once mingle, dance, have fun together freely and with unselfconscious abandon. Every young girl quite naturally dreams of being queen of this ball of all balls, the choice for once being made without regard to status and social origins. Arabella has been chosen; and she, the most beautiful of them all, seems to accept this unique tribute as something rather self-evident, due her as a matter of course. Her heart and her thoughts are elsewhere, for she has just been told about Mandryka and his intention to ask for her hand. Unaware of her father's rather shabby machinations which led up to it, she believes that their first meeting in the street was what made him fall in love with her.

As the curtain rises, she is slowly descending the flight of stairs that leads from the main ballroom to the hall. Mandryka watches her with breathless delight.

"Here comes an angel, descending from heaven," he exclaims, while Count Waldner more prosaically expresses his impatience with the lady, wanting to introduce the wealthy suitor as quickly as possible. Arabella, however, hesitates. She senses the element of irrevocable destiny in this meeting, and

though her turbulent heart beats wildly for this irresistible
Stranger, she cannot reconcile herself that easily to the surrender of her freedom and her maidenhood.

The parents leave the young couple to themselves. They
now confront each other for the first time, in the midst of
turmoil and confusion, but alone with one another as though
on a desert island.

Mandryka lacks words to express his feelings. He has none
of the easy grace bred into the urban aristocrat accustomed
to ballroom floors and the art of repartee. His passionate heart
is full to overflowing, but no platitudes come to his aid in
this predicament. Arabella is far superior to him in this one
respect, and she already has caught hold of herself. Aware
of his embarrassment, she is the first to break the troubled
silence. But instead of making things easier for him, she succeeds, on the contrary, in tangling them further. Her wholly
conventional question as to what has brought him here immediately unleashes a pointed challenge.

"Are you seriously asking me what leads me to this place,
Countess Arabella?"

Their conversation in the course of this scene is interrupted
several times by the other three suitors, each of whom persists
in asking for a dance, and is turned down consistently; Arabella has reserved this hour for Mandryka.

Mandryka, however, is upset by Arabella's apparent lack of
foreknowledge. Her father, it seems, has not told her anything.
He therefore, with a forthright and brusque directness, impatient of subtlety and circuitous compliments, abruptly comes
to the point after first briefly telling her the story of his life.
He had been married to a woman whom he loved very much,
but whom God took back, perhaps because she was too good
for this world.

Arabella listens in silence, sensing Mandryka's warmth and

utter purity, and for the first time experiencing her self-assurance as something this man, after his marriage to an angelic creature, must feel as disturbingly alien. (The singer of the role of Arabella must not, however, give the impression of resenting Mandryka's mention of his late wife as either tactless or intrusive.) "Is this, then," she asks him humbly, "what my father was supposed to have told me?"

Her gentle question brings him back to the present.

"Forgive me," he stammers. "I'm half a peasant; things with me move slowly, but with an irresistible force." And as he stands looking at her, his feelings break through like a dammed-up stream bursting its dikes. Even her mere picture already had seared his soul.

Arabella does not understand. Her picture? What picture? How could he have seen a picture of her way back in Slavonia?

Realizing that she knows nothing about her father's cheap intrigue, Mandryka deftly parries her question without answering it.

His words seize her like a storm in which she is caught, helpless; and yet she does not want to surrender without at least some token resistance. Never before has a man spoken to her with this fierce passion. She rises abruptly, and Mandryka perceives the glint of resistance in her eyes.

The humility with which he begs her forgiveness is not unmixed with bitterness. "Please forgive my unseemly speeches that keep you from dancing."

Arabella, however, sits out another dance and asks Mandryka to go on talking.

It is now up to her, she realizes, to bring them both back down to earth. She confesses candidly that she knows exactly what he came for, but adds that, before he makes up his mind to marry her, he ought to know something about her family and about herself. They are ruined and vaguely disreputable, little better than derelicts, leading what she refers to as a "shadowy existence."

Mandryka, however, is interested in Arabella and nothing else. He does not give a hang for form and conventions. His sole desire is to marry this beautiful woman, and in an impassioned speech he asks her to be his wife.

Arabella is profoundly moved. At last the man of her dreams has come to claim her, the one to whom she can belong body and soul, whom she will honor and obey.

Mandryka tells about a beautiful custom in his native Slavonia: when a girl in his village consents to marry a suitor, she brings him a glass of water in the evening as token of her chastity and everlasting devotion.

Overwhelmed, Arabella looks at him tenderly. At last a man different from all the others she has ever known, with a purity about him and about the very air he breathes! Mandryka exclaims that he will enthrone her as his wife, that she is to be his ruler, to rule wherever he is master.

The beautiful folk-song-like duet that follows is based on a Croatian tune, profoundly moving in its simplicity, though not nearly so simple for the singers. The soprano, in fact, must reach rather vertiginous heights:

so ge-be ich mich dir___ auf Zeit und E - - - wig keit.

The embrace at the close of this duet should be an especially tender one, with Mandryka gently taking Arabella into his arms, and his kiss must be a soulful promise of eternal bliss.

But Arabella abruptly changes her tone, switching back to everyday reality from the world of passion and dreams. Why does she check herself so abruptly? I believe that she cuts short the embrace simply because it suddenly strikes her that they are very much in the public eye—right near the main hall, liable to be surprised at any moment. This, at least, is the manifest, superficial reason as opposed to the true, far deeper one: for the first time in Arabella's life a man's lips have made her tremble, and she flees from inner turmoil into the shelter of outward conventions.

Now she would like to dance, take leave of the carefree days of her maidenhood. But when Mandryka tells her that he wants to stay with her, she already feels caught, her freedom limited, and he senses resistance in her hesitation. Quickly therefore he urges her to pay no attention to him.

The guests are arriving to claim the Queen of the Ball, and a folk singer, the well-known Fiakermilli, presents Arabella with a bouquet while singing one of her saucy ditties.

This Fiakermilli was a historical character who lived around the middle of the last century and enjoyed enormous popularity among the Viennese, who put pleasure above all else in life. Hofmannsthal's delightful idea of introducing her at his *Fiakerball* was a stroke of genius.

Arabella distributes the flowers among the guests and, as a parting gesture, tosses the last rose to Mandryka.

Countess Waldner is now talking to Mandryka. Zdenka furtively appears with the desperate Matteo, who cannot understand why Arabella never so much as gave him a sign of recognition. How is he to understand this? In vain poor little Zdenka tries to talk him out of his gloom by telling him that Arabella loves him just the same.

On both sides of the stage the action now unfolds which culminates in the terrifying climax of the second act. On one side are Matteo and Zdenka, on the other Arabella's parents, with the exuberant Mandryka, who wants all the world to share in his happiness and who makes plans for a gigantic party, with rivers of champagne and mountains of flowers. By way of making a start, he orders a wagonload of roses for Arabella to dance on.

Thereupon they all leave the stage to make room for the waiters who will ready it for the celebration.

Arabella appears, accompanied by her devoted swains to whom she now gently breaks the sad news, saying good-bye to each of them in turn. Lamoral, the youngest, receives a sisterly kiss on the forehead, which suffices to transmute his anguish into bliss. A last dance, and then good-bye forever to girlhood dreams and pleasures.

Beside himself with pain and desperation, Matteo breaks up this final waltz. He feels that this is the end of his hopes and assumes that the letter Zdenka is handing him contains word of the final breach.

Zdenka, however, has made the heroic decision to give herself to the man beloved by her, making him believe that she is Arabella. The envelope she hands Matteo contains the key to Arabella's room, where Zdenka herself will be waiting; in the darkness, while holding her in his arms, he will mistake her for Arabella.

Her decision has been made at the expense of great anguish and inner conflict: Zdenka's pride and virtue both rebel against this sacrifice. But her love for Matteo is boundless, and for his sake she will sacrifice her life, if need be. His happiness is the only reward she asks for.

The opera *Arabella* never has been very dear to my heart, and I suspect that this particular, implausible, and in fact wholly incredible situation has bothered me most of all. True enough, many operas are replete with improbable situations, and even *Der Rosenkavalier* is not convincingly realistic in its comedy of errors. But *Der Rosenkavalier* has so much charm and its libretto so much genuine wisdom that mere lack of credibility can be forgiven. In fact, I honestly believe that the libretto would have made a delightful comedy even without the music. I said as much to Hofmannsthal's son when I met him in London some years ago, and he exclaimed that he wished his father was there to hear me. "It would have made him very happy indeed; he was a very great admirer of yours, you know," he added.

I did not know, but I was most gratified to hear it, because Hofmannsthal never so much as said a word to me. He always attended rehearsals for *Ariadne*, but only as a silent observer. Perhaps he was an unduly shy person. At the time I simply thought that he did not approve of me, and I therefore was especially glad to be told otherwise, after so many years.

Matteo is carried away by ecstatic bliss; he still can scarcely believe that Arabella, the proud, aloof Arabella, has sent him the key to her room, the key to paradise. Unaware of Zdenka's embarrassment, he hugs the key to his chest and staggers off like a man drunk with happiness.

Mandryka, however, has overheard this conversation unwittingly and now is petrified with horror. Disengaging himself by dint of sheer will power from the icy grip of total numbness, he summons his servants, and in a fit of insane fury shouts imprecations, and barks out orders that manage to confuse everybody and everything hopelessly until at last one clear idea emerges—their lord and master, it appears, is looking for a man with a key.

Mandryka rages on, the untamed savage in him taking over. He hugs and kisses Fiakermilli, pours down drinks, insults the Countess, acts like a lunatic, and heaps sneers and innuendoes upon Arabella. Count Waldner, outraged, requests that Mandryka leave the ball at once and accompany them to question Arabella. With ironic politeness Mandryka complies.

With the arrival of Mandryka's guests, invited for the celebration, the act closes in utter turmoil.

Act Three

The lobby of the hotel. Matteo appears on the landing above, cautiously peering down. He would like to disappear discreetly, without being seen, after his strange and rather incomprehensible adventure, having just emerged from Arabella's room and the embrace of Zdenka, mistaken by him for Arabella.

Someone is apparently approaching the hotel door from the outside, and as the doorman goes to open it, Matteo quickly draws back. Through the door steps Arabella, returning from the ball, unaware of the terrible confusion, Mandryka's fury, Zdenka's sacrifice, and Matteo's bliss. She comes floating in, as it were, buoyed by waves of happiness, radiance personified. Slowly, as in a dream, she crosses the stage, almost dances across it, then sits down and begins to envision a future so rosy that she cannot quite bring herself to accept it as true. There will be fields and forests, Mandryka's vast estates, and he is the lord of it all as he is the lord of her heart. And she will be his mistress, his lover, his wife.

Matteo, who until now had remained concealed in the shadows, leans over the banister and is startled to see the woman he believes he just has left, sitting there calmly, dressed as though ready to go out.

Arabella is almost equally startled and asks him if this is where he lives.

It is Matteo's turn, now, to be utterly confounded—can she be serious, she who a mere few minutes ago was his up there in the dark room?

"Arabella, you," he begins, addressing her in the familiar second person as he had done earlier, in those moments of ecstatic bliss, "Arabella, you aren't going out at this hour, are you?"

The girl fairly bristles with indignation at his (to her) utterly incomprehensible behavior. In a chill reproof she explains that she has just returned from the ball and now wishes to go up to her room; dismissing him with a curt "Good night," she is about to leave when Matteo stops her. Hiding his confusion behind a false front of controlled fury, he tries irony. "Returning from the ball, eh? Going up to your room, eh?"

Baffling woman. How can she do this to him, after all that has happened between them? And so, trying once more to remind her, he steps closer. "Arabella," he whispers.

She is at her wit's end. Can he be drunk? How dare he speak to her in this tone of voice?

The whole episode, as I see it, is not devoid of humor; it is therefore of the utmost importance not to let this situation, meant to be deadly serious, slide into sheer travesty.

Matteo will not be intimidated. After all, he has proof positive of Arabella's true feelings toward him, and he is not going to accept this sudden reversal without protest. His male pride is wounded; he will not be toyed with by this girl, and so, heedless of her struggle, he attempts to embrace her by force.

At this precise moment Mandryka and Arabella's parents enter the lobby. The Countess vainly attempts to provide some harmless explanation for this embarrassing situation; Mandryka, immobile, stands paralyzed by fury. He has now recognized Matteo as the man to whom the key was sent, and when Arabella steps forward to greet him in joyful surprise, he coldly requests permission to leave.

Startled, Arabella looks at him. How could Mandryka possibly mistrust her? But her efforts at clearing up the confusion are quite as futile as those of her mother.

Count Waldner, however, refuses to accord Mandryka permission to leave; there are, he feels, misunderstandings at the root of this that need to be clarified at once, and only Arabella can help. And when she simply states that as she returned from the ball she happened to meet Matteo in the lobby, the Count considers the matter settled and closed. A girl like Arabella does not tell lies.

Mandryka, however, is deeply hurt. Far too worldly-wise to share the Count's simpleminded convictions, he is out now to inflict hurt in turn. Stepping up to Arabella, he promises to repair whatever damage money can repair; and, meeting her eyes, he wonders aloud how all this could possibly have happened.

Arabella assures him that nothing has happened, nothing she needs to be ashamed of, certainly nothing she would need to conceal from him or for which she would have to ask his forgiveness. It is she, in fact, who will have to try hard to forgive him for his lack of trust.

But Mandryka's reply is icy sarcasm. He is much too sure of himself, and the evidence of his own eyes and ears seems to him incontrovertible.

Matteo now intercedes, immediately making matters much worse. He declares himself ready to duel Mandryka to determine once and for all which of them has a right to Arabella.

"Mandryka has every right," Arabella exclaims, "and Matteo has none! None whatsoever!"

Matteo keeps his silence, but by his bearing and mien indicates that there are things about which a properly brought-up gentleman will not prattle in the presence of strangers. Arabella is utterly beside herself, for whatever else she may have thought of Matteo, she always had considered him to be a man of honor. Why is he lying now? What is this infamous game of his supposed to lead to? Is he simply trying to prevent her marriage and break up the troth?

Matteo himself is also caught in a terrible conflict. Being a gentleman, he under no circumstances wants to compromise Arabella; on the other hand, his mere silence is precisely the sort of reply that Mandryka interprets as a guilty plea. His voice charged with chill sarcasm, Mandryka in fact congratulates the lieutenant on his good luck with the ladies as well as on his exquisite discretion.

Arabella turns to her father, seeking protection.

The Count calls for his pistols, challenging Mandryka to a duel. The pistols, however, long since have been pawned.

The scene is about to approach its climax, and once again Strauss finds the spoken word more powerful than song.

"I have nothing further to say to you, Mr. von Mandryka," says Arabella, with forced restraint.

Richard Strauss's conception of this phrase differed from my own. He wanted these words uttered in a calm tone of voice, and I can certainly appreciate his thinking; he wanted Arabella portrayed as the imperturbable lady calmly rising above the situation.

However, I simply felt unable to speak the line in the manner intended by Strauss. I was far too intensely aware of the emotional pitch reached by both of these human beings, and I used to utter those words with teeth tightly clenched. Jerger, that marvelous Mandryka, reacted in one heartbeat. I was told that when he played this same scene with Viorica Ursuleac, he took his cue from her and handled it altogether differently, a sign to me of his superb artistry.

Strauss, in any case, was not the sort of person to insist on imposing his own concept upon that of a performer, provided the latter's approach was based on genuine conviction. When I protested that I simply could not act the way he wanted me to because it ran counter to my feelings in the situation, he wisely let me handle it my own way, though perhaps he disliked it.

Mandryka now chases his servants out to fetch the pistols, night or no night, even if they have to wake the pawnshop owner.

[115]

At this moment Zdenka arrives to provide the denouement, salvation, solution to all mysteries and misunderstandings. She has been a furtive witness to the whole scene and has realized the extent of the damage wrought by her sacrifice and boundless love. More dead than alive, she throws herself into Arabella's arms and confesses all.

Convincing situations are not an absolute requisite as far as opera plots are concerned. Matteo's instant passion for Zdenka, which makes him forget Arabella on the spot, smacks of the happy ending, come what may; but, even so, everyone is glad to see that Zdenka's sacrifice was not in vain, and that her great love is about to find fulfillment.

Arabella, of course, also is moved profoundly by the evidence of such overwhelming devotion. Her beautiful words flow straight from the heart, a heart that now has found full redemption in the understanding that love is not love so long as in self-righteous pride it shrinks from self-sacrifice and dedication.

"You, Zdenka, are the better of us two," she tells her sister. "You have the loving heart, and nothing in this world exists for you except that which your heart bids you to do."

And out of this newfound knowledge she holds out her hand to Mandryka, ready to forgive his lack of confidence, sensing for the first time the full measure of the hurt sustained by him and the fury it aroused.

Mandryka is thoroughly ashamed of himself, but Arabella's forgiveness makes up for everything. He now realizes that it is up to him to repair some of the damage caused by his rash behavior. Taking both Matteo and Zdenka by the hand, he leads them to the Count, and once again a scene of moving reconciliation takes place, whereupon the Count, much relieved, prepares to go back to his friends and his game. Mandryka and Arabella are left alone at last. Mandryka, conscious of his guilt, does not dare make the first move, and instead scans Arabella's face with tortured glances.

She, in turn, is now wholly in control of herself and of the situation. And instead of effecting a tearful reconciliation, she requests in the most amiably detached manner that he send up his servant to bring her a glass of water. "After this bout of conversation," she adds, with a shade of irony, "I believe I could well do with a glass of water."

She thereupon disappears, not deigning another glance in Mandryka's direction, slowly ascending while his eyes follow her every move.

As she disappears, Mandryka is left to brood over her words. She did forgive him, but how far does that go? Will she marry him after all? Did she want to tease him by asking for a glass of water? Let her; he'd rather be teased by her than ignored, and even her mockery is a grace he hardly deserves.

The music now quickens, and, on the landing above, Arabella emerges from her room, slowly descending the stairs and carrying a glass of water. Like the girls in Mandryka's own country, she is now coming to him, offering the symbol of purity and devotion.

This final, long, arialike speech of Arabella's is indescribably beautiful and makes the opera's ending an ever-new and gripping experience to me. Everything dissolves in harmonious and sensuous melody.

Mandryka, having drunk his fill, flings the glass to the ground. No strange lips shall ever again touch this glass—and nothing, no one, ever shall again come between Arabella and himself. She shall be his forever and ever.

Gently Arabella frees herself from his embrace and retires to her room, leaving Mandryka in a state of ecstatic bliss.

This is the beautiful end of the opera.

Der Rosenkavalier

WHEN I WAS a little girl and my good mother made
sandwiches for me with sliced radishes and salt,
I had a habit of subtly enhancing and pro-
longing the pleasure by pushing all the radishes to one side
of the bread and nibbling from the other end, gradually working my way toward the longed-for treat,
and finally devouring it all at once.

To have held off with the libretto of *Der Rosenkavalier*
is a somewhat analogous act of deferred gratification. I saved
this particular opera, so very important in my career as a
singer, to the very last in order to enjoy it to the hilt.

I very well remember when *Der Rosenkavalier* was first
performed in Hamburg. The year was 1911, and Edyth
Walker had been chosen to sing Octavian; in newspaper inter-
views right after the initial rehearsals, she voiced her delight
in Strauss's thoroughly enchanting music. She was a great
star in Hamburg and friend of First Conductor Gustav
Brecher, and her word carried weight in the world of music.
Max Lohfing sang Baron Ochs. Editha Fleischer-Edel was the
Marschallin, Elisabeth Schumann the Sophie.

Otto Klemperer had just at that time created a sensation in Hamburg as a conductor. Both he and Gustav Brecher had taken a friendly interest in me, and Brecher one fine day told me that I ought to study the part of Sophie because it was by no means out of the question that I might sing that role at the premiere. The remark happened to be unfortunate: it led me to believe not that I *might*, but that indeed I *would* be singing at the premiere. And so I learned the beautiful part, but, as it turned out, remained the understudy for Elisabeth Schumann, who sang it at the premiere. It was, of course, only right that she should; she was the most delightful Sophie imaginable, and far more skilled as an actress than my own (in those days) rather inhibited self. Besides, Edyth Walker had requested that Elisabeth Schumann sing with her, and Walker's word was law. That, however, proved small comfort to me at the time; I was utterly numb with despair. In one's younger days one is inclined to regard such disappointments as irremediable failures, and I walked around with a chip on my shoulder, fiercely hating our good Elisabeth who, of course, was wholly innocent of blame in the matter. A sterling character of translucent integrity, utterly incapable of even the least hint of intrigue and a truly devoted and faithful human being, she was later to become a great friend of mine; but at the time I darkly regarded her as a behind-the-scenes operator, and it came as rather an anticlimax when later on I finally sang Sophie, with Helene Brandes as Octavian, and earned a fair measure of success.

In due course I vocally outgrew the part of Sophie and became Octavian, a part I sang countless times with Elisabeth Schumann, first in Hamburg and later in Vienna, until a contract with Covent Garden in 1924 stipulated my singing the Marschallin, under Bruno Walter's direction. I signed the contract and learned the role within a rather brief span of time; but that, as it happened, proved to be merely the first step in mastering a task of astounding complexity. A good Marschallin has to be not only a good singer and a superb actress but also a many-faceted, sparkling human being, a great lady, a bewitching lover, and a conversationalist of the highest order.

Given the excellent cast, the most I could hope to accomplish in London was not to be conspicuously inferior. Delia Reinhardt sang Count Octavian in a manner charming and elegant, quite the "young scion" of an old aristocratic family coming of age as knight and swain of Sophie, a role that Elisabeth Schumann had made completely her own. Richard Mayr sang Baron Ochs, unforgettable and never equaled since; he succeeded in portraying this basically repulsive character with so much charm that one could never really be angry with him.

Each single role down to the very smallest was cast with the greatest of care, and the ultimate success of our London performance was such that it carried with it acclaim for my own individual contribution. Still, I do not believe that my Marschallin in those days came anywhere near my later interpretation of the role.

In order properly to appreciate this marvelous woman, one ought to be familiar with the beginning of the story.

Der Rosenkavalier — the Opera

Act One

*A*FTER A RIOTOUS prelude that describes with truly remarkable lack of reticence the pleasures of a night of love, the curtain rises upon a scene of peaceful intimacy: Marie Theres', the Marschallin, is reclining upon a couch in serene repose. Octavian, her lover, kneels by her side, his head in her lap while her hands gently stroke his hair.

This, at any rate, is the scene as presented on the stage, though actually Hofmannsthal had conceived it differently —with the Marschallin still in her bed and Octavian kneeling next to it. I do not know if prudery prompted this change in staging or a host of difficulties inherent in making this initial scene understandable in song. The bed cannot be discreetly relegated to the background, but should be conspicuous without dominating the stage; the audience should be aware of it. When I sang the Marschallin in Berlin, the young and *avant-garde* stage director in charge had the bed placed right in the middle of the stage; later on it was simply screened off. But throughout the scene with Octavian, it constantly seemed to be getting in our way, and I finally came to regard this arrangement as no solution at all. The *Rosenkavalier* premiere occurred in the days of the Kaiser, and the Imperial Court ordered a thoroughly "decent" staging of the opera which required omitting many of Baron Ochs's overly obvious insinuations. That first performance may, in fact, have been responsible for the continuing triumph of the so-much-more-"moral" couch over the all-too-obvious bed. The music of the prelude, of course, also should have been suppressed or expurgated to conform to Imperial standards of decency; fortunately the Emperor and his moralistic censors appear to have been deaf to its brash implications.

The Marschallin has become enamored of a young man, in fact still a boy rather than a man, and taken him as her lover. She is a woman *entre deux âges;* Strauss thought of her as being approximately thirty-five, the age at which, in that period, a woman begins to stop being young.

Marie Theres' is the wife of the Duke of Werdenberg. In that day and age, where even under the very nose of Her most exceedingly moralistic Imperial Majesty Maria Theresa the upper classes behaved in a scandalously depraved manner, no striking significance attaches to the fact of her having a lover. To have an affair was, so to speak, part of belonging to the right circles, and the Empress stood alone in her opposition to that universal licentiousness, quite unable to prevent it.

The Marschallin, then, is a woman well versed in the pleasures of love. Married off to her Field Marshal at a rather tender age, she had to wait for illicit affairs of the heart in order to discover the joys utterly lacking in her marriage. Now, on the very threshold of middle age, half resigned to it already, she takes pleasure in the boyish seventeen-year-old Count Octavian, who in turn has with her the very first adventure of his life. He, of course, thinks of himself as desperately in love with her; the night just past seems to hold out the promise of many more like it; and in his puerile megalomania he believes himself to be the first and only one who ever came truly to know the woman in his arms, the first and only man ever to arouse in her the sort of passion whose fruit he just has tasted. The Marschallin smiles indulgently at this display of juvenile naïveté. She has had many a lover, and Octavian to her is but a delightful pet, a darling boy; introducing him to the art of love has been a rather delicious adventure, but now she feels a bit tired, fatigued by his youthful ardor. Her whole behavior, therefore, should be governed by this pleasantly tender and relaxed fatigue. In answer to his dreamy-eyed remark that "No one knows, no one will ever guess how you were and how you really are," she playfully wonders if that is cause for complaint. "Would he want many others to have known?" Her use here of the formal third person singular is meant to indicate that she has switched back to an aloof conversational manner, while Octavian, still blissfully unaware of any changes, goes on addressing her in the familiar second person, once again assuring her as well as himself that he alone has ever truly roused her passion, that he alone knows "what she is really like."

Passionately he embraces the Marschallin, who tolerates the gesture without actually taking part in it; then, with characteristic abruptness, Octavian leaps over to the other side and, half prone, resting on his left elbow, begins to philosophize and to articulate some of the ideas that have passed through his head in the course of these intoxicating days and nights. "You and I—what do they mean, these words? We're one, are we not? And yet here I am longing for you, coming to you. What am I to you? Your boy, your very own; and yet, when we embrace, am I still a boy who belongs to you, or are you a woman who belongs to me?"

The Marschallin listens to him, a smile on her face; she is fond of this charming boy, who not only possesses all the natural virtues of his youth and beauty but who also can be tender and thoughtful, poetic and contemplative. Embracing him, cradling his head on her breast, she breaks into a song that begins on a low note and rises to a broad forte: "You are my darling boy, I love you." All of the maternal love a mature woman feels for this youngster is contained in her tender "You are my darling boy." But something else reverberates in that phrase as well. He is her lover; and the sweet, very warm "I love you" rises out of this troubling conflict of emotions. Tenderly they embrace.

Octavian rises at the sound of birds chirping outside; their song interweaves with the orchestral part in a delightful pattern. For a moment the Marschallin seems numb; covering her eyes in a fleeting gesture of fatigue, she drops her hands again, laughing tenderly as Octavian draws the curtains in order to prolong the night and stay the light of day, which threatens cruel separation. Octavian, quick to take offense, instantly demands to know if by any chance she is laughing at him, but the Marschallin smilingly calms him with words that once again set him off on a fit of passionate oratory. "Angel mine," he explains, and is about to fling himself into her arms when she brusquely stops him with a gesture indicating caution. She is listening to a far-off sound, some cruel intrusion marring the idyll of this sweet hour. Octavian refuses to acknowledge it. He will not have it; but the Marschallin goes on listening just the same. It seems to her that she can hear the faint, harmonious tinkle of the tiny bells that decorate the turban of her Moorish servant. She is not the least bit worried; no one, she knows, would dare to enter this room without her permission. But Octavian uses the opportunity to tease his beloved by rattling off a lengthy list of her suitors and admirers. "Might it not," he suggests, "be a courier with a note from Sarau or a servant with a letter from Hartig, or a billet-doux from the Portuguese ambassador?" He is, of course, jealous of them all and has good cause to be resentful; but at this particular mo-

ment he can well afford to thumb his nose at them all. Right
now he is the undisputed conqueror; and this proud sense of
superiority makes him stand there, arms crossed on his chest,
challenging all comers. "No one," he declares, "will cross this
doorstep without my permission. I am the lord and master of
this place." Lord and master, indeed—so much so that he has to
go hide as breakfast is being brought in. The Marschallin is
intensely aware of the comic aspects of the situation, and her
"There he goes, quick as lightning, hiding from the breakfast,"
is sung on a note of tender mockery. Octavian disappears behind a set of curtains which seem to conceal either an alcove
or a dressing room, and in his haste forgets to take his sword,
now conspicuously in evidence by the side of the bed. The
Marschallin sees it just in time, and in a flash of temper has
the boy retrieve it.

Throwing a robe over her negligee, she remains in the background while the little Moor, prancing prettily, wheels in
her breakfast and serves it to her on a small table. She waits
for him to leave before stepping again into the center of the
stage, though certainly not out of regard for the servant, her
page, her obedient shadow, who has many a time served her
breakfast in bed in compromising circumstances, and who has
seen her in negligee. There is no reason for her to be squeam-
ish about showing herself, and I cannot see the Marschallin—
as the scene often is played now—discreetly withdrawing behind a screen in order to slip into her robe. She moves toward
the rear of the stage simply because the robe happens to be
lying there, and after the Moor's exit she signals to Octavian,
who comes rushing out at once and wants to take her into his
arms. She, however, takes him by the ear and, tenderly mocking, drags him out to the footlights, mildly berating him for
his negligence; one does not leave his sword in a lady's bedroom. The boy needs to be taught some lessons in good manners; love is great, but he must also learn how to dissemble his

feelings. Octavian, however, unconscious of the laughter in her voice, is crestfallen at once, acutely embarrassed and guilt-stricken for having acted foolishly. All those others whom minutes earlier he had poked fun at—"Sarau and Hartig and the Portuguese Ambassador"—would have acted correctly, with proper polish, and never for one moment would have aroused the ire of their loved one. He strides to the opposite end of the stage and, putting up a show of truculence in order to hide his mortal embarrassment, questions their whole relationship.

"After all," he declares, "if you don't like the way I act, and if you aren't aware of the fact that I have no experience as yet in such matters, then I don't know what you see in me." She listens to him with a cryptic smile on her lips. True enough, he has "no experience in such matters"; but that is part of his charm, and his boyish clumsiness marks a welcome change from the artful supersophistication of which she has grown so tired. "Stop philosophizing, lover," she cries out tenderly, adding with a piquant emphasis: "There is a time for love and a time for food. This is the time for breakfast." Another lesson to be absorbed by Octavian—the art of waiting, of knowing when to be passionate and when to be tender, when to make love and when to make conversation. He still must learn that the intermission is also an important aspect of the play, overture and epilogue to the great comedy of love.

At this instant the Marschallin wants nothing more than sated repose. Worn out, she wants to start the new day with keen, refreshed senses, the night fading into a delicious memory. Octavian is obviously enjoying this breakfast together, another novel experience. With tender jesting and joshing he waits on his beloved, but so ardent is his youthful passion that it makes even this delightful interlude appear intolerably long. Taking the cup from her hand, he embraces her passionately, and they begin to whisper sweet nothings into each other's

ears; he calls her Bichette, while she in return has named him
Quinquin. But in the midst of this graceful love play he suddenly is struck by the awesome realization that here, still half
a child, he has become the lover of this most desirable of
women. "And to think," he exclaims, with childish pride, "that
at this moment the Field Marshal is hunting bear and lynx in
the forests of Croatia, while I, youngster that I am . . . what
am I hunting? God, I am lucky." His triumphant naïveté is
rather tactless, and mention of the Field Marshal makes the
Marschallin frown sternly. She does not approve of his making
fun of her husband, whom she fears and respects even though
she does not love him. To be cuckolded by a mere slip of a boy
would be a severe blow to a man's pride. In their social set, of
course, no stigma attaches to adultery; the entire Imperial
Court could be counted upon to understand and sanction their
respective behavior—always provided that there is the face-
saving fiction of "not knowing" about one's partner's affairs.
It is therefore exceedingly bad form to mention the husband
while making love to the wife! And furthermore, what does
this youngster know about a man like the Field Marshal?
He'd better not say another word on the subject. She herself,
of course, has every right to complain about her marriage as
loudly as she pleases and declare that it has brought her no
happiness; but that is none of his business, and he certainly
should know better than to bring up this touchy subject. Her
"Leave off the Field Marshal" is therefore an explicit reproof,
evoking a dream that tormented her during the night. "I
dreamed about him . . ." she adds languidly, disturbed and
absentminded now, caught up in fear for one brief moment; if
the Marshal really came to find out about it, if he were to appear suddenly, the boy would be silenced soon enough.

Octavian, however, never having known such a thing as a
bad dream or a nightmare, completely misunderstands the
purport of her remark; as far as he is concerned, it simply

means that while she was in his arms, she dreamed of her husband. He is both hurt and indignant; but the Marschallin, amused at his naïveté, does nothing to soothe his feelings. "I don't order my dreams," she says, smiling, gleeful at seeing him jealous now of the very man he so blithely mocked seconds earlier. His rising question, "This night, this very night, you dreamed about your husband?" becomes almost a threat, parried by the Marschallin with a light repartee. But when she goes on to tell Octavian that in her dream the Marshal suddenly and unexpectedly returned home, a cold shiver runs down the boy's back. He hardly knows the Field Marshal, having seen him very briefly only once; but he was instantly awed by the commanding manner of the man, and the sense of power he exuded well may have provided an added touch of piquancy to Octavian's conquest. For in his innocence, Octavian sees himself as having "conquered," whereas in effect he merely was chosen. But now, in his mind's eye, there rises the forbidding figure of the Field Marshal, and he would like to hide in a corner to avoid those cold, flashing eyes.

In answer to his whispered question, the Marschallin tells him all about her dream, in which her husband came back suddenly with all his retinue, invading the house and causing unbearable noise and commotion. But even as she tells about it, real noises from the yard impinge upon those recollected from her dream, and the Marschallin starts up in manifest agitation. Could it be that the Marshal really has returned, now —could it? He had not planned to return so soon, but, then again, how many times has he changed his mind abruptly and done exactly the opposite of what he had started out to do? Octavian, however, succeeds in calming her fears. "I do hear something," he affirms. "But it doesn't have to be your husband, does it? Just think of where he went; Reizland is way beyond Esseg." Marie Theres' knows nothing of geography; like all true "ladies" of the time she is blissfully innocent of any and all knowledge and is educated only in matters of etiquette. She has no idea of the distance, and when Octavian describes Reizland as very, very far, she sighs with relief. "Well, then, it must be something else."

But fear still veils her eyes as she keeps watching the door; the commotion on the other side of it seems to be coming closer. And when Octavian asks her, she is quick to admit it: "You know, Quinquin," she says, "the Marshal is swift as the wind." Both fear and pride are reflected in her voice, for she is after all a soldier's wife, and boldness, chivalry, love of adventure are in her very blood. If her husband has disappointed her as a lover, he still never has failed her as a soldier, a strong and fearless knight of the sword. She has boundless admiration for those qualities in him, and the phrase "The Marshal is swift as the wind" reflects this. She now remembers how he once caught her in a situation very similar to this one—how he *almost* caught her, that is; if he had, there could have been no thought of forgiveness. To this day she can still feel in her bones the abysmal terror of that moment and cherish the memory of her own quick-witted adroitness, which in the nick of time salvaged an all-but-irretrievable situation. She would like to tell Octavian about it in just the way she would have told it to a close lady friend, but something stops her—awareness, that it would constitute a severe *faux pas* to relate this particular adventure to a boy who persists in believing that he is "the only one." Suppressing a smile, she rebuffs his insistent questions with a kind admonition to be a good boy. "You don't have to know everything, after all." Octavian, on the other hand, is troubled by her reticence, wondering if there are secrets that she will not share even with him, the Only One, the Chosen One, the Victor to whom she belongs. He is determined to find out what it is all about. "Bichette," he pleads, "what was it that happened, once upon a time? . . ." And when she persists in her refusal, he flings himself upon the couch. "This, then, is how she toys with me," he cries out, in utter despair, plunged from the heaven of joy straight down into a hell hitherto unknown, the hell of jealousy.

The Marschallin, however, now pays scant attention to Octavian's histrionic fit of despair. The voices in the antechamber grow louder, quarrelsome, and it sounds as though someone wants to force entry into her bedroom, with the servants vainly trying to stop him. No one would dare even to contemplate such a brash deed—no one, that is, but her husband.

The Marschallin, thinking fast, puts an end to Octavian's pouting with a quick, "It's my husband." The words rouse Octavian from his mood. Grabbing his sword, he rushes to bar the door. Too late; the antechamber already is full of visitors and petitioners who would love nothing so much as to see a scantily dressed young man rushing out of the Marschallin's bedroom, sword in hand. What a juicy morsel for the Viennese scandalmongers!

The door in the center of the room also leads to the antechamber, so that the only action possible is to hide behind the bed curtains. But Octavian's daring love of adventure has been roused, and he refuses to go into hiding like a coward; he wants to be a man, to fight for his beloved, sword in hand.

The Marschallin is anything but delighted at this display of manly courage. The last thing in the world she needs from this youngster is his protection. Impatiently shoving him behind the curtains, she resolutely draws herself up, determined to deal with the Field Marshal in her own way. "Eyes flashing," as Hofmannsthal directed, she now stands at the door with her arms crossed. "I'd like to see," she declares, "if anyone has the nerve to come in here against my orders. I'm no Neapolitan general; when I make a stand, nothing will move me." Now she is all the soldier's wife, bold and daring. Her true self comes to the fore as she listens delightedly to the servants trying to keep out the unwelcome intruder. They all love and adore her and, doubtless well aware of the embarrassing situation, are eager to help. "Fine lads," comments the Marschallin, beaming approval. "Fine lads indeed. They don't want to let him in. They keep telling him I'm asleep." Taking a few steps toward the footlights, she deliberates on what to do next and decides to meet the danger head on, open the door, welcome the Marshal with an audacious show of innocence, and find out how much he knows and what he has to say. Perhaps he already will know all about Octavian; rumors may have reached him. Perhaps this is the end. Very well. So be it. Marie Theres' is a fearless woman who has tasted happiness when it has come her way, has enjoyed every moment of it, and now is ready to pay the price, whatever it may be.

Resolutely she steps to the door, ready to meet her husband. At that climactic moment she hears the voice of the stranger, and the whole burden of conflict and terror drops from her at once. "Oh, Quinquin," she shouts, "It's only a visitor"—and her words are the *Auftakt* to a delightful Viennese waltz. And in waltztime she continues to wonder aloud, pert and carefree now, who the visitor might be. "My God, it is the Ox," she exclaims, "Baron Ochs von Lerchenau, I mean, my cousin. Now whatever could he be wanting from me, at this hour?" And it occurs to her that a day earlier, as she was sitting in her carriage by the side of her young lover, a messenger delivered a letter from Baron Ochs which she, preoccupied with her charming Quinquin, never bothered to open. How could she possibly have found time to read a letter from this most repulsive of cousins. But now he is here, undoubtedly in connection with something mentioned in that stupid letter, and she has not the faintest idea what it is all about. It is all Octavian's fault, as she laughingly informs him.

But as she turns around, Octavian is nowhere to be seen. Why does he still keep hiding, now that the danger is past?

In the meantime, however, Octavian has slipped into the chambermaid's dress that he found in the alcove, and is beginning to enjoy the whole situation thoroughly. Aside from the fun of the thing, the whole notion of disguising himself strikes him as eminently clever: dressed as a chambermaid, he certainly should be able to slip out unnoticed, certainly more inconspicuously than if he had left the Marschallin's bedroom as Count Octavian. There are a great many servants about the house, and no one is likely to question his business or his identity. Of course, he ought to have left much earlier, at the crack of dawn, in which case he would have been seen only by the soldiers detailed to guard the Marschallin. Those soldiers were a discreet lot, ready to look the other way. That undoubtedly would have been far more intelligent than to linger till all hours; but who the devil can be intelligent when he is in love with a woman like Marie Theres'? So passionately in love that he just cannot tear himself away?

This charming disguise, Octavian believes, will solve all his problems; but he obviously cannot deprive himself of the pleasure of letting Marschallin in on his act. With short, graceful steps he comes prancing out from behind the curtain, greeting the Marschallin in the Viennese argot. "At your service, Your Excellency. I'm new in this place . . ." Marie Theres', laughing delightedly, holds out her hand which he immediately seizes and starts to kiss avidly, quite unlike any chambermaid. In return, all she is able to give him for his nimble-witted inventiveness is a quick kiss, together with the urgent behest to come back soon—"but in men's clothes, and via the front door."

Octavian is about to rush out when the door swings open and Baron Ochs enters, arrogantly snarling at the servants who are still attempting to hold him back.

Baron Ochs . . . How can I go on writing without letting my thoughts wander and return to Vienna and Salzburg, to the immortal memory of Richard Mayr. Others have sung and played the role of Baron Ochs with distinguished success, and I might even have considered them ideal—had I not known Richard Mayr. Mayr was Viennese, first and foremost, Viennese in what one might call the cozy, comfortable sense of the word, and at the same time an aristocrat. Roughhewn, a country squire, for all that he always was surrounded by an aura of "class." And when he came crashing into the Marschallin's room, the incident became not just a case of peasant crudity, but an action symptomatic of class consciousness displayed by a nobleman to the manner born, unwilling and unaccustomed to being put in his place by yapping servants. Richard Mayr lucidly conveyed the whole range of meanings. No matter how often I sang with him—first as Octavian and later on as the Marschallin—he always delighted me anew, surprising me with the many-faceted subtleties of his portrayal, the charming improvisations, the irresistible gaiety of the warm personality that in the end made even the repulsive Baron Ochs come across as a basically lovable character aglow with precious humor. Mayr actually transformed the Baron into a boorish character, a boozy, dilapidated spendthrift whom no one could really hate because he was so pathetically funny at heart. His was an inimitable, a onetime portrait that simply cannot be copied. No one is irreplaceable, and Baron Ochs has been sung by many others successfully, credibly, and with superb effectiveness; but to me the inimitable personal note with which Mayr managed to endow the figure of Ochs has been missing ever since; and I never sang the Marschallin later on without being sadly reminded of Richard Mayr, a great and valued friend fated so early in his life to leave this world, which he loved so much.

Baron Ochs, then, forces his way into the room and, in doing so, collides in the doorway with Octavian, who is hastening to depart. The Marschallin regards this unexpected and undesired turn of events with evident concern; the actress representing her must take care to leave the center of the stage immediately upon Octavian's exit, as she is not the principal figure in the following scene and must not obstruct the audience's view of Ochs colliding with Octavian. Ochs now occupies the center of the stage, making a conspicuously pompous entrance. The Marschallin, about to withdraw, stops at the sight of the two people colliding, but then, a moment later, walks on, sitting down at her dressing table in the background and beginning to powder herself, stopping from time to time to watch Baron Ochs.

The Baron, who had been in such a hurry to see the Marschallin, now appears to have all the time in the world, and the pretty young chambermaid seems of vastly more interest to him than the dignified Marschallin. Contrary to all the rules of etiquette, therefore, he devotes his attention exclusively to this presumptuous chambermaid, whom the other servants eye with puzzled consternation: they never have seen her before and seem mildly startled at finding a new servant in attendance. Octavian plays his role to the hilt, twisting and squirming as the noble lord addresses her, and vehemently shaking her head when asked if she has hurt herself.

The Marschallin at last slowly turns around, determined to put an end to Octavian's dangerous game, and the servants, already dismayed by the Baron's insolent behavior and lack of common courtesy, now quietly but insistently remind him of her presence. "Her Excellency is waiting . . ." Baron Ochs immediately proceeds to greet the Marschallin with due and proper form, while with a polite smile, she informs him that he is looking very well indeed—a conventional phrase that the Baron instantly insists on taking literally. Preening himself, he once again reproves the assembled servants for having barred his way. Now the Marschallin is annoyed. No guest has the right to address her servants in this manner. Furthermore, she is not accustomed to having men ignore her presence while they dally with the chambermaid. Frowning angrily, she leads the Baron to the front of the stage while her eyes seek out Octavian, who in turn is thoroughly enjoying this mad situation. He rather likes himself in the role of chambermaid and tries to avert his face as much as possible from the curious eyes of the servants; therefore he busies himself in the background, fussing around with the bed and furiously fluffing up the pillows. Though aware that he ought not to be drawing the Baron's attention to himself, he so relishes this delightful comedy that he simply cannot help himself, and, disregarding the Marschallin's angry and reproachful looks, behaves in the most conspicuous manner possible. He is still very much the child, and this is a game he does not want to stop playing.

The Baron now involves the Marschallin in a conversation to which she listens with only half an ear. She intensely dislikes her cousin, is annoyed at his intrusion, and for her merely to remain civil requires almost superhuman effort. But then a remark of his to the effect that he often pays such early morning calls upon the Countess Brioche captures her attention, for an aura of scandal always surrounds the Countess, and Marie Theres' is both interested and amused to learn that she received Ochs while sitting in her bathtub, protected only by a flimsy screen.

The Marschallin orders the servants to bring in some chairs, and Ochs watches as they leave the room, reminded once again of all the trouble they made for him. He would have liked to see them punished for their audacity; after all, he had announced his visit. The letter that the Marschallin never had bothered to read indicated the date and hour of his arrival, giving every right to assume that the servants would have orders to admit him. Marie Theres' offers her apologies and explains that she had been suffering from a headache all morning, while her eyes, roaming, seek Octavian, who blows her a graceful kiss from the alcove. He still is reluctant to leave, hoping that Baron Ochs will depart in short order and leave the field clear for another round of love. Instead, the Baron also turns to seek Octavian, just a fraction of a second too late to see the kiss. The chambermaid looks good to him, and, without consideration for the Marschallin, who continues to complain of her headache in a vain effort to get rid of him, he settles himself on the couch that Marie Theres' offers him with very obvious resignation. She realizes that he is ogling the chambermaid constantly, and therefore lightly mentions that the young thing is just fresh from the country and a bit on the clumsy side. "If she bothers you . . ." She is looking for an excuse to send the boy away formally and officially and thus put an end to his stupid game, which is beginning to get on her nerves; can't he understand that he ought to disappear as expeditiously as possible? For sooner or later Baron Ochs is bound to meet young Count Octavian, and it would prove more than embarrassing if at that point he were to recall the features of the young chambermaid—the more so because Ochs is just the sort of person who would come right out and express his astonishment in public. The Field Marshal has a shrewd mind and an eagle's eye; he would put two and two together in no time, with tragic consequences for all concerned. The Marschallin, therefore, is not amused by Octavian's irresponsible joke, though deep down she appreciates his grace and skill as a comedian.

Baron Ochs feels constrained to explain his manifest interest in the pretty little girl before him; after all, he says, he is now engaged to be married. The Marschallin expresses genuine startled surprise, whereupon the Baron seems baffled in turn; he had explained the whole situation in his letter, hadn't he?

That unfortunate letter . . . The Marschallin has some difficulty in not laughing aloud, and now feels called upon to do a bit of acting herself in order to make the Baron tell her what was in that letter without becoming aware of the fact that she never had read it. Who, she asks, is the chosen one—"the lucky one," as she puts it with scarcely veiled sarcasm. Ochs, busy ogling Octavian, pays scant heed to her questions until a curt and explicit demand makes him respond. "Fräulein Faninal," he replies, angry now at the Marschallin for making him repeat information contained in his letter. Yes, of course, he is well aware of the fact that this marriage is a *mésalliance* from the point of view of his class: Herr Faninal is a *nouveau riche*, his is hardly the sort of family one marries into, and Ochs assumes that the Marschallin's pointedly failing to remember the name is an expression of her disapproval of his impending marriage. Matters seem to be taking another turn for the worse when the Marschallin inquires further about the family. "They're not local people, are they?" The poor woman merely is trying to find out what the letter contained, and has no idea that the intent of her questions is being misinterpreted radically. Ochs is furious. With pointed emphasis he explains that the Faninals are local people indeed, "raised to the peerage by grace of Her Majesty." Marie Theres', as it happens, is not the least bit interested in the Baron's affairs; listening with a feigned show of interest, she watches Octavian, who has become bored staying passively in the background and now has emerged, preening himself provocatively right in front of the Baron's nose. The Marschallin, incensed at this thoughtless and irresponsible behavior, frowningly tries to signal to him with her eyes to get out as fast as possible, to make himself scarce. But Octavian is in a high and irrepressible mood, and nothing in the world can stop him now. He is in love, more than ever in love with the Marschallin, and he likes to watch her make conversation *à la grande dame* with this nincompoop of a baron, while at the same time the anger in her beautiful eyes melts from time to time and yields to a flirtatious warmth destined for Octavian alone.

Baron Ochs, perceiving the Marschallin's manifest distress, mistakes its cause for something altogether different and believes her to be indignant at his wanting to marry a commoner, or rather a newly titled girl, which in a sense seems almost worse. He therefore tries to rationalize the *mésalliance*; after all, she ought to understand his position even if she is swaddled in the traditions and conventions of her class to the point at which she can forgive no minor deviations. The father of his prospective bride happens to be incredibly rich. The girl herself is as radiantly beautiful as an angel and just has been graduated from convent school. Her father owns half of Vienna and is said not to be in the best of health. . . .

The Marschallin listens, anything but amused; she visualizes a pretty young girl forced by a ruthless and ambitious father into a marriage that is bound to be a miserable farce at best. She knows her cousin for the low-down, vulgar wolf he is, not ashamed even in her presence to flirt with a chambermaid. Fleetingly, she feels sick at the thought of his marrying an innocent young girl; and he still thinks *he* is the one that is lowering himself and committing a *mésalliance*.

However, this is none of her business, and she is not going to mix in his affairs. Things like that happen all the time, all over the world. The world, in fact, is full of people like Baron Ochs and wealthy Herr Faninal, and nothing can be done about it or about the way they act.

She therefore sidesteps the issue by uttering a platitude on a note of jesting complicity. "I'm catching on at last, dear cousin. I'm beginning to see the light." Slyly winking, the Baron proceeds to make plans for the children to be born of this marriage; they will obviously not have true blue blood coursing through their veins, he admits, but his own status is so exalted that it cannot fail to be reflected in the standing his wife and children will acquire at Court. And while his childen may never be able to wear the golden keys of a marshal, an honor restricted to those of untainted noble lineage, they will be happy and content with the twelve cast-iron keys to the twelve houses owned by Herr Faninal.

The Marschallin is beginning to find this outspoken naïveté rather hilarious, but Octavian, bored to distraction, finally has decided to comply with the Marschallin's silent request. He picks up the tray with the breakfast dishes and is about to depart, but instead of going quickly and inconspicuously, he deliberately chooses to provoke the Baron's interest all over again by prancing off right before his eyes.

Baron Ochs reacts promptly and precisely as the impertinent youngster had wanted him to. Recalling the chambermaid, he all but blackmails the Marschallin into offering him breakfast, which she, torn between laughter and rage, finally does. Ochs now proceeds to divide his attention equally between the Marschallin, whom he addresses in a highly formal conversational tone, and the apparent chambermaid, whom he is determined to seduce. Thus he interrupts the story of his impending marriage by whispering promises and urgent requests into Octavian's ear, to which the latter responds coquettishly with impudent mimicry. In spite of herself the Marschallin has to laugh; pretending not to notice the game being played by the Baron, she asks with studiedly courteous interest whom he has chosen as his Bearer of the Rose, a figure in an ancient custom of great ceremonial importance: the groom, before appearing in the presence of his bride, sends her a noble knight bearing a silver rose as token of his love.

As it happens, this problem is precisely the reason for the Baron's visit; no one in his immediate family would seem of sufficiently exalted birth to qualify as his Rose Bearer (*Rosenkavalier*), and as he had stated in his letter, he would like the Marschallin to suggest the proper person. Oriented at last, the Marschallin rapidly ticks off the possibilities: Cousin Preising? Cousin Lambert? She will have to think it over, she finally declares; she will give him the name the next time they meet.

The Baron, however, is insistent, and presses for a dinner date the following day. But now Octavian is up in arms, gesturing furtively, protesting that he has priority. He wants what he wants, and what he wants is to be with her tomorrow and the day after and the day after that and all the days thereafter . . .

Marie Theres' disregards his carryings-on; her main concern at the moment is to get rid of the Baron, and her pointed question as to whether there is anything else she can do for him is plain enough. The Baron, of course, is wholly impervious to such a subtle hint, and, as it develops, also would like to have a recommendation to the Lawyer, a most important problem because it involves drawing up the marriage contract, that crowning achievement of his labors which will deliver his bride's fortune to him. The Marschallin contemptuously smiles at his obvious eagerness and wants to seize the opportunity to send Octavian away as inconspicuously as possible without further fuss. She therefore asks him to send up the Lawyer, always in attendance in the antechamber at this hour of the morning; but she has underestimated Baron Ochs's pigheaded persistence. "I would never," he crows, "let such a golden child mingle with the lowly servants." To which the Marschallin can only reply that he is really too considerate.

Enters Struhan, the Majordomo, a figure of impressive dignity with whom the Marschallin gets involved in an intricate conversation that gives the Baron a chance to draw Octavian aside and to try to arrange for a tryst with his "sweet little chambermaid." When cooingly he asks if she has ever had a tête-à-tête with a boy friend, Octavian coyly shakes his head; and when Ochs suggests a date, Octavian, in the broadest Viennese dialect, wonders out loud if "it's right to obey." The Majordomo and the Marschallin have their backs turned, but the Marschallin, even while checking letters and petitions, keeps track of what goes on, secretly amused by Octavian's brash game.

I would like here to insert a remark concerning this scene: it can be carried too far by Octavian very easily. The actress portraying him never should forget that Octavian is of noble birth, that grace and good manners are innate in him, and that he is actually incapable of carrying out in practice the vulgarity he is attempting to caricature.

Quite often this is forgotten; the actress starts to clown for the audience rather than staying within the framework of the subtle comedy that constitutes the very essence of *Der Rosenkavalier*. For example, the crude gag of having Octavian, half dragged onto a chair by Ochs, kicking up his legs in a deliberately clumsy fall is, in my opinion, evidence of decidedly poor taste. In the first place, the Baron certainly would not permit himself such blatantly coarse behavior in the presence of the Marschallin; such flirtation as he does engage in should remain strictly within plausible limits. Furthermore, Octavian certainly should know how to twist out of the Baron's embrace without resorting to the to me always embarrassingly vulgar trick of lifting his legs way up in the air, an unseemly, crude joke that is out of place in this opera.

With barely suppressed hilarity, then, the Marschallin follows the progress of the flirtation between Octavian and Ochs. Dismissing the Majordomo, she reclines gracefully in an armchair and observes with mock politeness that Cousin Ochs does not seem to disdain delicate morsels.

Ochs is clearly relieved to have his outrageous comportment judged so mildly. For a moment he had come close to being embarrassed, worried lest his cousin come right out and tell him exactly what she thought of the way he is behaving.

Charming woman, really; *femme du monde*, one who forgives and forgets, not to mention understands. Kissing her hand, Ochs pays her what he considers a compliment for being so utterly devoid of sanctimonious hypocrisy.

Half in jest, however, the Marschallin reminds him that he is about to be married and that this is hardly the way for a man in his position to carry on. Whereupon the Baron, irked and provoked, insists on enlightening her as to his notion of love; in great detail he describes the veritable and real delights of love as both the Marschallin and Octavian listen, their amusement mixed with a soupçon of outrage.

The Marschallin rather maliciously interrupts to inquire if the Baron regards this so-called "love" as a full-time occupation, and he proudly affirms that he does: "What other occupation is there," he asks, "that would be more in keeping with my status?"

This exceedingly long discourse by Ochs is often cut drastically. The Vienna version retained much more of it than is customary anywhere else, and I even recall that at one point we tried a completely unabridged version. But it tends to become wholly unmanageable and much too long unless the Baron Ochs happens to be sung by someone like Richard Mayr.

The Baron, then, ends his starkly colorful description of the joys and pleasures of love with vivid instructions on the conquest of bashful dairymaids; and in order to provide the proper illustrations, he clutches Octavian and attempts to kiss him. The scene closes with a fast, light trio. Octavian, slipping out of the Baron's hot hands, with a sigh of relief rushes over to the Marschallin, who is convulsed by the turn of events and obviously feels that a kiss from the Baron would have served Octavian right as proper punishment for his impertinence. When the Baron formally requests that she let him have the chambermaid as servant to his future wife, she finally gives

way to her pent-up hilarity without further inhibition. She
is particularly delighted by the Baron's unrestrained praise
of the maid's natural good manners. There must, he asserts,
be a drop of blue blood in those veins. "You have keen eyes,"
she acknowledges, exchanging an amused glance with Octavian, Count Rofrano, the bluest of the blue bloods indeed.
Ochs has great understanding of the family complications of
the nobility; he himself, in fact, is attended by a valet who also
happens to be his own illegitimate son, a fellow by the name
of Leopold. Leopold will deliver the silver rose to the
Marschallin, who can take that opportunity to get acquainted
with a son of Baron Ochs.

The Baron's idle chatter about "blue blood" and his illegitimate son suddenly gives the Marschallin an idea: she will
show him a picture of Octavian, hoping that he will immediately notice the resemblance to the chambermaid. This, in
turn, will give her a chance to explain that the chambermaid
in all likelihood is an illegitimate daughter of Count Rofrano,
thus preventing future complications, because Ochs, if and
when he does meet Octavian, no longer will find anything
very remarkable in the resemblance and will remember instead
what the Marschallin has told him about the illegitimate affair.
In fact, she now plans to arrange for a meeting between
Octavian and the Baron as soon as possible, while he still
remembers her story, and for this purpose she now proposes
Octavian as the Rose-Bearer.

Octavian, unable to perceive, let alone to understand, the
subtle intrigue being spun by the Marschallin, is horrified at
the order to bring her his picture, but does as he is told. After
all, she knows what she is doing. . . .

Lovingly the Marschallin takes the locket with Octavian's
picture, a beautiful portrait rendering the seductive, youthful
charms of her lover in all his grace and manliness. For quite a
while she sits there, lost in contemplation; then, lapsing into

an easy, conversational tone, she inquires whether Ochs might not perhaps want this young gentleman as his Rose-Bearer. The musical phrase flows freely in waltztime, hinting at the sweet memories dancing in the Marschallin's heart, and all her love reverberates in her explanation, "My young cousin, Count Octavian." The words should be made to sound like a caress; then, as though having suddenly made up her mind, she hands the Baron the picture, and he starts in amazement. "What a resemblance! . . ."

The Marschallin draws a sigh of relief, her stratagem having proved successful. Bubbling over with hilarity, she affirms that she herself often has wondered about it, and then goes on to inquire slyly if the Baron happens to know old Count Rofrano, the brother of the Marchese—"No, not Octavian's own father, but rather the second brother. Well, it seems . . . we understand each other, don't we?" And so, knowing the chambermaid to be of noble birth, she always has kept her somewhat apart from the others, as something special. Rising from her chair, the Marschallin lovingly draws Octavian close to her. "Always by my side . . ."

But now she has had enough; deceiving the Baron was work enough for one day. With dignified and wholly indisputable authority, she dismisses Octavian. "Go on, now, Mariandl, and send in the others." Octavian, paying no heed to the Baron's feeble protests, lets out a ringing "Come in all of you" in broad dialect, and grabs a cleaning woman, waiting with mop and pail on the other side of the door, shoving her into the Baron's eager arms, thus ending the latter's pursuit.

The Marschallin, chuckling over the incident, now retires to the dressing room, followed by her servant. The morning ablution in those days was a rather symbolic affair, consisting of a tiny bowlful of water, a towel, and enormous quantities of eau de cologne. It seems passing strange in retrospect that in an age of extreme cultural refinement and delicate taste very little attention was paid to matters of simple cleanliness, and we may perhaps do well not to look too closely into the hygienic practices of those days so as not to blemish the image of the Marschallin. Suffice it to say that the ceremonial of the makeup was far more extensive and thorough than the process of merely getting clean; and every morning the rites of makeup, followed by the even more involved and artful engineering feat of constructing the towering coiffure, were, so to speak, in the public domain. This was the time when petitioners, tradesmen, peddlers, savants, and artists crowded the Marschallin's antechamber and were admitted to her august presence.

The commotion on the stage is now further enhanced by the arrival of a pet dealer bringing puppies, monkeys, and a parrot.

This part of the scene has led to many a hilarious situation, and I always used to look forward to the arrival of the pet dealer, who as a rule brought a different dog with him each time. The animals gave us so much trouble that for a while in Vienna we kept a senile, lethargic mongrel so far past any interest in what was going on around him that he would huddle quietly in the dealer's arms and blink diffidently at the audience. Shortly thereafter the monkey had to be dropped from the repertoire because his enterprising showmanship proved altogether too diverting so that the tenor found himself hopelessly outclassed in competing for the audience's attention.

At one time Elisabeth Schumann, the delightful Sophie, sent me her Pekingese, named Happy. It was wearing a huge purple bow, happily wagged its tail when called, and insisted on jumping onto my dressing table, much to the delight of its mistress. I also had an adventure with a Pomeranian that had come to us directly from the kennel three days earlier and still was deadly afraid of everything and everybody. My maid, whom I had brought with me from Vienna to America, was standing backstage at the Metropolitan that night holding sweet little Mausi in her arms. For some reason, as it developed, no dog had been sent us for the pet-dealer scene. The stage director, seeing Mausi, simply snatched the animal from the maid's arms, delighted to have found so easy a solution to the problem. The maid, who spoke practically no English, could neither understand his explanations nor explain in turn that the high-strung little dog would probably expire of fright on the stage. No one paid the slightest attention to her desperate efforts at communication, and moments later I suddenly faced an utterly petrified Mausi out there on the stage, sitting immobile as a monument in the dealer's arms, too frightened even to recognize me.

A far more disconcerting problem was dogs that would wag their tails wildly, leap delightedly at the Marschallin, and try to snuggle down in her lap. Personally I always enjoyed this scene enormously, because in my almost pathological love for animals I never do seem to get enough of them around me, no matter what the situation.

But I have been getting ahead of my story. The Marschallin comes out of her dressing room and is greeted by the assembled company with a deep bow, acknowledged by her with a gracefully benevolent smile as she walks past the bowed heads toward her dressing table. This mixture of absolute aristocratic superiority and charming benevolence constitutes the very essence of the Marschallin's character: she embodies the ancient Viennese tradition of being "democratic" in a highly aristocratic manner. The true Viennese aristocrat never can be really arrogant; his charm and casual nonchalance are such as to make even his presumption of innate superiority seem lovable. The Marschallin settles at her dressing table and concentrates on her makeup, aloof from the routine commotion that now starts all around her.

An Italian tenor, furthermore, who has been waiting to sing an aria, seems disturbed by the presence of all these strangers, whom he clearly assumes to be far beneath him in social position. He would like the famous Marschallin to pay exclusive attention to him. The actress should, by the way, greet him, and him alone, with a gracious nod. After he begins to sing (*"Di rigori armato . . ."*), she should stop to listen to his song from time to time—a gesture lacking in most of the performances that I attended. For whether or not the Marschallin likes music, whether or not she actually enjoys the tenor's contribution, happens to be beside the point: she is a woman of transcending charm, a large part of which consists precisely of her convincing way of demonstrating interest in other people. She likes the singer. At the next opera performance she will be sitting in her box, and the good-looking tenor will be singing for her alone.

When the first part of the aria is over, she graciously applauds, and then has the Majordomo bring the tenor to her so that she can utter a few flattering remarks. The tenor gratefully kisses her hand and withdraws, turning to his flutist in obvious excitement. Here he ought to convey the impression of giving an enthusiastic account of how delightfully charming the Marschallin had been to him.

She ought to be equally amiable, though in somewhat more aloof and absent-minded fashion, to the tradesmen offering their wares. The actress here must find a way of devoting concentrated care to her toilet while doing justice to all those around her clamoring for her attention.

When the Baron shocks all those present by reviling the Lawyer in a vulgar outburst, the Marschallin's first concern is the tenor: his aria has been interrupted, and he has been insulted under her roof. She therefore turns to him with an apologetic gesture, and he rushes over to kiss her hand. I have seen performances in which the Marschallin at this point handed the tenor a purse, but in my opinion a lady of the Marschallin's exquisite sensitivity would not act in so crass a manner. The tenor, after all, is not a beggar, and though artists were not regarded as altogether acceptable in those days, this charming woman is ready to make an exception. A brief glance in the direction of the Majordomo suffices to convey her instructions, to be carried out discreetly later on. All that she herself now offers by way of reward is her outstretched hand and a gracious smile.

Today she finds herself thoroughly dissatisfied with her hairdresser and repeatedly expresses disapproval with the way in which he has set her coiffure. Her face in the mirror looks tired, wilted by a night of stormy caresses that, while they lasted, made her feel happy and young as she had not felt for many a night. But now, in the cold light of morning, she must pay for it by having the cruelly truthful mirror face her with the image of a woman getting old. She still refuses to admit this to herself, and therefore blames the hairdresser rather than the passing years. Interrupted by a noisy outburst on the part of Baron Ochs, who is arguing with the Notary somewhere in the background, she is about to terminate the session, and casts a final glance in the hand mirror. "My dear Hippolyte," she chides the hairdresser, "today you've made me look like an old woman." It is extremely important to render this phrase with the correct expression. Above all, it should not be uttered on a note of vehemence or as a severe reproof. Rather, what reverberates in these words is all of the Marschallin's helpless resignation, veiled by the pretense of injury. It must be delivered with quiet resolution. The Marschallin thereupon flings down the mirror on the dressing table with barely suppressed anger. She *acts* the role of the injured party, the mistress not properly attended to, the spoiled lady unaccountably neglected, but deep in her heart she already has come to understand that the blame does not lie with the hairdresser and that no one maliciously has transformed a woman in the prime of life into one looking older than her years. She knows it, realizes it, and her anger is nothing but a last futile effort to avoid facing that knowledge.

With frantic eagerness the hairdresser now attacks the artful coiffure before him and attempts to improve on what was well-nigh perfect to begin with. But in a sudden fit of impatience, the Marschallin abruptly dismisses those present. She, who as a rule has a friendly word for everyone, today confines herself to a curt order.

As the people slowly file out and a conspiratorial Italian couple, Valzacchi and Annina, smelling business, engage Baron Ochs, the Marschallin tries to improve her appearance by means of pearls, rings, and brooches, discarding them as fast as she picks them out. Sad and searching, she stares at the large mirror, heedless of her surroundings.

As a rule a learned scholar is at this point made to appear on the stage, presenting a huge tome to the Marschallin, who politely leafs through it and indicates condescending appreciation. Personally I am not fond of this gimmick, which smacks too much of filling a vacuum. At any rate, I always experienced it as distracting rather than helpful, and in my opinion the Marschallin ought to be left completely to herself at this point. The whole scene, after all, is a marvelous preparation for the beautiful monologue, and the less she is distracted by external happenings, the better it seems.

An actress would be inept indeed if she could not convey by means of facial expressions what is going on inside her. True enough, opera houses are vast, the audiences rather distant from the stage, and one might be led to think that facial expressions would tend to get lost, so that simply sitting still would be bound to seem lifeless. I see this problem in a different light. I believe quite firmly in wavelike radiations emanating from the performer and making their way to the very last row of the house. It may be the power of personal magnetism that holds the audience spellbound; I do not know enough about these things to discuss them authoritatively. But I do know that the secret of "personality" goes deeper than a fleeting and momentary effect upon a receptive audience. Just as some people can tame wild animals by the mere look in their eyes, so certain performers can captivate an audience by their power of expression, whether it be quelling a disturbance or overcoming a lack of attention. When I sense a commotion in the audience, a certain disquiet, the shuffling of feet, coughing, rattling of paper, and the like, I never blame anyone but myself. The fault is mine; I failed in my mission. There is no such thing as an inferior audience; the only one inferior is the artist incapable of holding his audience. This he must be able to do even on the stage of a vast opera house, and the spell cast by him must be felt even if the actor's features cannot be perceived in minute detail. Furthermore, tension is conveyed by stance and attitude; the body is so subtle an instrument for the expression of thought and feeling that it would seem almost difficult *not* to communicate what is so plainly self-evident.

Thus at this point the Marschallin ought to be sitting alone, very quiet, almost motionless, her thoughts and emotions mirrored only by her face.

Eyes reflective and sad, she is seated before her mirror, looking at the jewels in her hands. And even those hands, for all the tender care they receive, are betraying her, for hands above all will unfailingly reveal a woman's age even while a thousand beauty secrets keep the face still looking young and fresh.

Obviously in any scene where several actors share the stage, it is imperative that the director's instructions be obeyed by all. There can be no exaggerated individualism, and one person must assume responsibility for the overall effect. As a rule I used to avoid making suggestions; for some reason, directors invariably seem insulted whenever a singer shows evidence of having ideas of her own, and the greater a reputation I acquired as an opera singer, the more assiduously I endeavored to fit in smoothly with the team and keep from turning into the dreaded prima donna. I always was able to express my individuality and my personal conception within the framework of the overall production, and making a virtue out of this necessity became in fact an artistic challenge. The ideal solution is for the singer to thresh out all differences with the director beforehand and arrive at a common approach, but this depends on the working methods of the persons involved. As for myself, I never came to a rehearsal with a preconceived notion of how I was going to act; instead, I always let myself be carried away by the inspiration of the moment. I firmly believe that what alone matters is a truly complete grasp of the part as such; the kind of basic understanding I have in mind renders irrelevant such minor problems as external mannerisms, gestures, and position on the stage. For this reason I always complied with the director's wishes and instructions unless they happened to conflict in a really fundamental way with my own ideas.

In Vienna we had an excellent director in Wymetal, to whom I owe a debt of gratitude for his unflagging attention. He closely followed every performance, severely criticizing any bad habits or awkward movements that would creep in. Maria Jeritza's highly developed sense of theatrical effects was to him a source of special gratification, and I recall how he once told me that she was like clay in his hands. "All I have to do is give her a hint," he said, "and right away she carries it out, giving form and expression to everything that was in my mind at the moment." In those days Jeritza was under his constant care and attention, and his impeccable taste suitably restrained her tendency toward excessively acrobatic histrionics. I remember many performances in which she had moments of breathtaking beauty. Her Tosca was superb, and her singing the prayer while lying on the floor was a genuine and deeply felt inspiration rather than an eccentric affectation. And at that time, when her hair fell down over her face, the effect was electrifyingly natural. Later on, however, when she was remote from Wymetal's influence, that shock of hair always coming undone at precisely the same moment began to seem awkward and embarrassing because the artifice, the practiced gesture with which she removed her bobby pins, became so obviously contrived as to vitiate the illusion of tragic pain. Wymetal used to watch her with relentless severity and eliminate without mercy anything smacking of stage effects.

Wallerstein, though very wise and knowing, had a tendency toward overacting. He brought a much-needed breath of fresh air into the atmosphere of the Viennese opera, but his modern ideas had not been tested in the fire of experience. I had lengthy arguments with him when he first arrived, but in due time our struggles resulted in a peace based on mutual respect, and later on I came to enjoy working with him. I do believe, however, that to the very end he never liked the idea of my not doing everything exactly the way he wanted it done. He had a way of turning pale on such occasions, and I could see the effort it cost him to control his anger. "Here you go again, turning yellow around the nose," I used to tell him, and as a rule this standard joke between us would break the spell. He was a man who could teach a great deal to anyone willing and able to learn without surrendering his freedom. "If a singer can also act," he once told me, "people call him a genius—what personality, what brilliant ideas! But just let him be dull and clumsy, and right away it's the fault of the director. How could he let the fellow go fumbling around like this? . . ." There is much truth in the remark, for the director unquestionably is the hardest-working person backstage during rehearsals, and the one whose efforts were least appreciated.

Times have changed. Today the stage director seems to be the star. The singer generally stands motionless, almost becoming a part of the orchestra so to speak . . . "Symbolism" is the main theme of the whole.

To me opera is always *living drama.* The more the singing actor or actress is able to bring a role to life, the more they have fulfilled the purpose of opera singing and acting. Even if the libretto shows little opportunity to make the plot and the acting plausible—even then it should be the foremost task to try to *be human.*

Of course I know that nowadays one has very different ideas about stage settings. One cannot do it anymore in the same style as in Richard Wagner's lifetime. One has to modify, to simplify. But this kind of "objective art" which seems to be the new way is to me lifeless and cold. It almost seems to be *old-fashioned* instead of new: the singers *sing* and don't *act.* Everything is stripped of humanity, becoming symbolic, stark, and without charm.

When I came back from Bayreuth some years ago, I was quite confused. I said to my very revered friend Bruno Walter: "If this is the new way, then I should stop teaching. Because I feel everything so differently. What good can it be for my students if they learn to act as I see it—and then, joining opera houses in Europe, they suddenly are confronted with such a different conception that it must deeply confuse them." Bruno Walter answered—and reassured me: "This so-called modern way of acting can only be a phase which will vanish. What you teach is based on tradition. Let the students learn this tradition under your guidance—it will be for them a good basis on which to build up their own conception."

That made me continue to teach.

One ought not to exaggerate the role of the stage director.

Someone once pointed out to me that if the director plotted every movement and position ahead of time, then everything the singers would do by way of acting would become mere imitation, the sole originally creative person being the director. This is sheer nonsense. No two people ever do exactly the "same" thing, and a truly gifted performer always will stand out in any pattern. He may take advice from the director, may even let himself be persuaded or influenced, but within the rigid framework of the preconceived pattern he always will stand out and go his own way.

Whoever wholly identifies himself with someone else's ideas is not a personality in his own right.

Toscanini, Bruno Walter, and Strauss left a performer free to himself so long as this freedom was based on art. It would be counter to the very essence of art to enslave what needs freedom to unfold.

But I have come a long way from the Marschallin; let us return to her now as she sits sadly brooding before her mirror. Groping her way back to the reality of her immediate surroundings, she notices the two Italians in animated conversation with Baron Ochs, and cuts them off by rising. Some productions manage to make it appear as though the Marschallin is getting up because the Baron is addressing her; needless to say, this is an outrageous blunder. Quite on the contrary, the Baron turns to her because she is getting up, thus conveying her desire that the conversation be terminated.

Baron Ochs wants to introduce his illegitimate son, whom he mentioned earlier, and the Marschallin manages a distracted, mirthless smile as the Baron refers to his ridiculous-looking offspring as "the counterpart to the pretty chambermaid." The hideous creature delivers the silver rose in a huge red box, and the Marschallin, with barely concealed irony, compliments the Baron on his son and heir.

Above all else she now wants to be left alone, alone with her thoughts, so that she can try to come to terms with what so deeply wounded her awhile before—the sudden awareness that her days are growing shorter, that the summer of her life is gone, that surrender and resignation lurk in the shadows. When the Baron requests that she call in the chambermaid again, she suppresses a smile; instead, she curtly refuses, but reiterates her promise to obtain the services of young Count Rofrano as the Baron's best man. "He'll do it for my sake," she says, and again a vision of the young girl forced into a hellish marriage with this repulsive cousin of hers rises before her mind's eye, causing her to put an end to the interview. "And now, good-bye." She has decided to go to church to seek absolution from the understanding priest to whom she has many a time confessed the sins of the flesh. Quickly crossing the stage, she watches the Baron's departure.

Alone at last, she now can drop the mask of politeness, which on this of all days seems more oppressive than ever before. She despises Baron Ochs, this low-down creature who is putting out filthy tentacles to crush an innocent girl. And with that he still has the colossal impudence to insinuate that *he* is the one who is lowering himself.

Suddenly the Marschallin is trembling with rage. In great excitement she starts back to the other side of the stage, but stops short abruptly, her sense of humor getting the better of her and restoring her perspective. "After all, what am I getting worked up about? This is the way of the world. . . ."

A rather lengthy prelude, this, to the superb monologue, and the less "acting" the Marschallin does, the better. The thoughts that move her are not of tragic profundity, being merely a restatement of her basic philosophy, such as that one has to take things as they come, and that nothing is ever as bad as it seems. The bride of Baron Ochs also will manage to survive somehow, will settle down after exhausting the resources of tears and rebellion, will become a good wife, will raise a brood of charming children, and will grow more realistically modest in her expectations.

Or else, and more likely, she will follow the pattern customary in her social circle, have extramarital affairs, find happiness in someone else's arms, sin, do penance, and be forgiven. Why get excited? That is life.

What the Marschallin should be doing here is standing quietly, half-smiling, pensive. She has learned to smile the wise smile of a woman tried and tested by life, the smile that, carved out of youth's passionate rebellion, is one of life's greatest and most gratifying victories. Thoughtful, she should walk over to her dressing table and sit down, hesitant, brooding. She very definitely must avoid conveying the impression of sadness; the music here is joyfully moving. Her thoughts merely *touch upon* past and depressing times, when she herself was unhappy in a prearranged marriage. But all that has receded into the dim, distant past, has been clarified and resolved, and now is remembered only as one remembers a sentimental song of yesteryear, a trifle sad, perhaps, in a sweet, warmly pleasant way.

The Marschallin recalls her own girlhood, the day when she herself, just barely out of convent school, was forced into a marriage not of her choosing. With a melancholy glance at the mirror, she seeks that youthful image of herself. "Where is the girl I used to be? Where are the snows of yesteryear?" Just barely past childhood, still dreaming and hoping—and here I am already about to grow old. The very notion seems absurd, and the Marschallin simply cannot conceive of herself as cold, extinct, gone—she, who this very night was young again in Octavian's arms, the torrent of passionate life coursing through her veins as never before. And yet, soon no one will whisper passionate pleas into her ears, the deaf ears of an old woman. Bowed by the weight of the imagined years ahead, she imitates the people talking to each other about her. "See that one over there? That's old Duchess 'Resi. . . ." There is something frightening about the idea, and in sudden panic the Marschallin grips her throat. How can this be? I am unchanged, the same as ever, with the same strong heartbeat, the same passions and desires, the dreams I dreamed as a child, even if the faces and the songs around me have changed. I am what I am, and I don't want to turn into a living corpse.

God alone knows why it has to be this way; but why do I have to see and feel it coming, with full awareness of what is happening to me? Why can't I just imperceptibly slip from one age into another, simply accepting this as the natural course of events? Certainly I've learned to understand, but there are some things I'd rather not understand, and this is one of them. I don't want to be robbed of life's beauty and warmth, have it slip out of my grasp while I still am fully conscious of what is happening.

God, my God, I don't understand You.

Perhaps Your ways are meant to remain hidden to us poor sinners. We simply have to accept and bear them.

This serene wisdom now marks her smile as she lifts her head. "It is the *how* we accept and the *way* in which we bear it that makes the difference," she whispers in what sounds almost like a warning to herself. She is determined to accept old age with dignity, to resign herself to the inevitable. This is her philosophy of life.

Octavian, now in a smart cavalry uniform, enters the room, and the Marschallin glances up in startled surprise—not so much at seeing him as at the realization that she had come close to forgetting all about him. He has seemed so far away.

Here the actress portraying the Marschallin should not neglect an apparent trifle, that of drawing the robe more tightly about her. She should, as it were, put up a facade and get set to face the world again, where a moment earlier she had surrendered completely to the luxury of loneliness, letting the robe slip off her shoulders. It is daylight now, time for formal dress. "There is a time for everything . . ."

Looking up at Octavian, she smiles in friendly greeting. He comes storming in, flings gloves and cap on a chair, and is already by her side, eager once again to take her in his arms. There is a time for love . . . And at his age, the time for love is always. The Marschallin, however, gently fends him off; she is sad and tired now, unable to act the radiant lover. Octavian, noticing her sadness, is moved by it to sweet, tender solicitude. He is proud as well, convinced that her sadness is part of her having been frightened, having feared for his life. In his youthful egotism he ultimately manages to refer the Marschallin's every word, glance, or action back to himself, anxiously trying to convince himself that nothing else in the world exists for her and that, if she feared her husband's sudden return, it was because of fear of what might happen to her lover. His heart is overflowing with happiness and gratitude, but when he wants to clasp her to his bosom again, she wards him off with a tender gesture, shaking her head. What a lovely boy, and how sweet his faith that he alone now matters in her life. Half-mocking, she admits to having been somewhat worried about him while secretly reliving that moment —what if her husband really had come home? No point in being afraid. She always will look danger straight in the eye and take the consequences for whatever she has willed, desired, or enjoyed.

Octavian laughingly reminds her of the subsequent course of events, when the door opened and Baron Ochs appeared. "Some field marshal," he says, again antagonizing the Marschallin by this tactless reference to her husband, a man whom she respects while at the same time she wants to forget him. Therefore she rather coldly rejects Octavian's advances and would, in fact, prefer his leaving altogether. She feels sad and tired and wants to be alone. For the moment play and laughter, passion and fire are things of the past. He ought to understand; but he is selfish and ruthless, no different from other men. Tiresome, this always having to relive the identical experience with one man after another, this routine of letting herself "be conquered," which she has come to despise. And now this mere slip of a boy, whom she herself chose as a lover, already is convinced that she belongs to him, that she has become his property by virtue of her having let him make love to her for a night or two. He already wants to play the lord and master, and she, in turn, is much too jealous of her freedom not to resent this. Irritated, she upbraids him for being just like all the others. But the effect is rather startling, for instead of countering with some hotheaded remark of his own, as she both feared and expected, he merely utters a sigh. "I don't know what all the others are like," he says miserably. "All I know is that I love you."

To him she seems changed in a puzzling and disturbing manner, and he blames it on all the annoying intrusions, the crowds of importunate strangers who invaded the room all morning. How could she let them come between him and herself? Once more he is deeply unhappy, and the Marschallin, both touched and charmed, holds out her hand in a gesture of reconciliation which bears clear traces of irony—he, the proud, would-be possessor, is mere wax in her knowing hands. Octavian, sensing the import of the gesture, wants to go further, but she resolutely stops his advances, withdraws to her dressing table, and then leans on it, facing him. She would like to tell Octavian about her feelings, would like to make him understand, and therefore tries to talk about the fleeting nature of time, the quick passage of days, months, years, life. Everything, she concludes, dissolves in your very hands, everything you want to hold onto turns into a dream. . . .

But Octavian, a young man on the very threshold of experience, cannot yet grasp the tragic aspects of life. He finds it utterly incomprehensible that she, this radiant, happy creature, should waste her time brooding over the future instead of living in the glorious present. It can mean only one thing: she must be tired of him, for otherwise, if she loved him the way he loves her, she could not be capable of such dark thoughts. Weeping, he flings himself into a chair, while the Marschallin looks down upon him with a troubled smile. "Be a good boy, Quinquin," she admonishes him, talking as though to a child and stroking his head, keenly aware at the same time of the grotesque aspects inherent in the situation. "Here I still have to comfort this youngster because sooner or later he is going to leave me . . ." She utters these words tenderly rather than in a spirit of reproof, but Octavian, incensed at the note of superciliousness, rises abruptly. What has come between them? he demands to know. Why has she changed so much since the break of day, and who is it that speaks with her voice? For this surely isn't the Marie Theres' who lay in his arms all through this night of all nights.

The Marschallin pays no attention to his outburst. Slowly she moves back to the dressing table and sits down all through the beautiful monologue on time. What she is trying to make Octavian understand is that time not only transfigures the external world about us, but is at work within ourselves as well.

We live, insensitive to its constant flow; but a day comes when suddenly we are confronted with the evidence of its power—the day that marks the beginning of the end, the passage of the peak, the slow descent into death. And from that day on we begin to worry about time, to watch it anxiously, to become aware of it in our very bodies, running out like the ineluctable flow of sand in the hourglass. We see time in our face, in the mirror, everywhere, moving, passing. With a heavy sigh the Marschallin turns to Octavian. "Sometimes, Quinquin," she says, her voice husky with emotion, "I can hear the passage of time, ticking away without mercy." For time is silently undermining their love as well, no matter how ardently they may wish to halt its ravages. Lost in her thoughts, the Marschallin thus is led to avow fears that she never has admitted openly to anyone else, but the confession is made almost as though she were unaware of his presence. "Sometimes, you know, I get up in the middle of the night and stop all the clocks and watches in the house. . . ." But how can he be expected to understand the nature of this fear, he who is as fleeting as time itself, here today and gone tomorrow, far away, remote in his love and devotion, his fickle heart elsewhere? Time, that most implacable of enemies, lurks in the shadows, biding its hour. And the hour is near, the parting imminent. The Marschallin sits up in sudden terror, listening to the ominous footfall of time, time that will not be deceived by stopped clocks and watches.

But she suppresses her fear. "On the other hand, one ought not to be afraid of time, either," she remarks, with a gentle smile. "It, too, was created by the Father of us all." There we have it once again, the mature wisdom of life, the ready acceptance, the quiet surrender—"For such is life"—expressing deep comprehension and joyful acquiescence in everything God has seen fit to bestow upon mankind, be it happiness or pain.

Octavian listens attentively at first, but soon is made to feel uneasy by her speech. He understands perfectly well everything she is trying to express; but why the deuce does she insist on dwelling upon these somber, melancholy topics instead of letting his kisses wipe away whatever fear and unhappiness are troubling her? Every last one of her thoughts should be exclusively concerned with him, just as he imagines himself to be living exclusively for his beloved. She ought to forget about time; what is time, anyway? What are mere years when measured against the boundless magic of a woman such as the Marschallin? After all, she is infinitely more charming than any young girl he has ever met, and he wants no lectures from her about impermanence and resignation. Tenderly approaching her, he takes her hand in his; love alone is what makes him wonder why she should be giving in to these black thoughts just when he is with her.

In a flash the Marschallin realizes that this is the moment for her to tell him clearly and precisely just what the end is going to be between them. She wants him to know that she anticipates that end calmly and with no fear in her heart. She does not want him to feel bound to her by fear or remorse, does not want him to cast her the crumbs of his love as cruel alms. Time, the wrecker, shall be left to do its work.

She turns to him, taking both his hands into hers. "Quinquin," she begins, "either today or tomorrow you'll leave me for another, one younger and more beautiful than I. . . ." Richard Strauss directed that the words "more beautiful" be sung with "some hesitation," a very feminine touch expressing the fact that a woman would find it harder to accept a rival's greater beauty than her merely being younger. Youth, after all, is a natural and unearned merit; Octavian is bound to tire sooner or later of an aging woman and seek happiness in the arms of a younger one. But as for beauty, the Marschallin always has been outstandingly beautiful, and it hurts to come up against the ineluctable truth that her beauty is fated to wilt, that she must make room for others. Slowly, haltingly, she walks away from Octavian, crossing the stage toward the left. Octavian desperately protests that all she wants is to get rid of him, that she utters these horrible prophecies merely to drive him away, to make him understand that she simply no longer loves him.

The Marschallin keeps looking out of the window, not trusting herself to meet Octavian's eyes. "The day will come all by itself, Octavian," she says, feigning casual indifference;

she is in love with this youngster, in love with him as the very embodiment of youth. He symbolizes passion, laughter, carefree living, and grace. But now he begins to assail her with fierce reproaches. Tomorrow means nothing to him; today is what he is interested in, and above all he wants her to stop tormenting him. With a sob he sinks to his knees, clinging to her.

This scene is frequently staged in such a manner that the Marschallin, while talking, moves to the left behind the couch, and Octavian in turn throws himself onto it, with her standing behind him and leaning over as she goes on singing. I have strong objections to that particular arrangement and always have played the scene differently, taking the very center of the stage and standing erect, with Octavian kneeling at my feet. For what the Marschallin next has to say is the absolute climax of the first act, and for her to say it while hiding behind a couch seems ludicrous to me. Even from the purely visual point of view—one never to be disregarded—the Marschallin must have the center of the stage and not be half-concealed by a couch.

With explicit emphasis the Marschallin now repeats her prognosis. Today or tomorrow or the day after—but happen it will. It is bound to. He will leave her, and what she wants him to know is that she expects it to happen, that she wants him to go his own way. No, she is not telling him this in order to torture him, but merely because it happens to be the truth; and the warning, if such it be, is addressed more to herself than to him. For he stands to lose nothing. He will stride on out into the sea of life while she remains behind, lost and deserted. This ruthless foreknowledge of doom is what spurs her on to seek ways of coping with it, for anything in life can be borne if one has learned to accept the facts of defeat and disaster rather than holding on desperately to something that no longer can support the weight of one's hopes. The important thing is to be serenely relaxed about taking as well as about losing, to receive the gifts life has to offer in full awareness that, whatever they be, they are a loan rather than a gift in perpetuity. Only those able to make peace with this transient aspect of life can avoid fatal wounds. God, the Creator of the universe, also has created time and wants us to understand its nature. We must work out our own problems, and we can do so only by recognizing them as part of life's task.

Octavian is profoundly upset. How can she be trying to ease the pain of parting when the mere thought of it is more than he can bear? Why part if there is love such as theirs, love that will last through all eternity? She has no business to be talking to him like a preacher in church about God and punishment and mercy. He is not the least bit interested in such topics and wants to talk about love rather than philosophy. "Does that mean," he wonders, passionate and hurt, "that I shall never be able to kiss you again?" The Marschallin nods, herself hurt to the quick. Yes, the time will come when he will cease to kiss her, kiss her no longer till her dying day. And she will never again drink from the fountain of life, touch these beautiful lips. The end will come soon, brought about by time flowing in their veins—in hers far more cruelly than in his. She is tired of passion and turbulence, longing already for loneliness and serenity. She therefore wards off his embrace and, when he shows signs of not wanting to reply, becomes sharply explicit. "I wish to be left alone," she says, with an authority that brooks no contradiction.

Octavian gives up, realizing that neither pleas nor tears, neither passion nor tenderness will get him anywhere. He no longer is wanted. She has asked him to leave. Silent, he waits for an instant; but when the Marschallin announces her intention of going to church, he collects his sword from where he left it behind the curtains and truculently buckles his belt.

The Marschallin meanwhile has sat down again at her dressing table. The morning, as she now plans it, will be devoted to certain duties and obligations sadly neglected of late for the sake of this charming young lover of hers. There is the church, first of all and most important. Her good priest will be expecting her and will hear her confession as he has heard it so many times before, and then she will leave the church an altogether new and different woman, stronger, cleansed of sin, renewed. Immediately thereafter she will pay a visit to old Uncle Greifenklau, whom she has not seen for ages, and will accept his invitation to lunch—a dreadful bore, but conceived as penance of a sort for all the delights she recently has enjoyed. After all, that new and different Marschallin leaving the church will have to think of doing some good deeds; the priest will insist upon that, and letting herself be half bored to death by old Uncle Greifenklau should count as a very virtuous act indeed. Oh, how long the hours will seem, whereas with Octavian they pass in a flash. She casts a glance at him; the boy looks hurt, sad, and fierce. Perhaps she will be able to see him in the afternoon; she could send him a message if she decides to take a drive through the Prater. And if so, it might be fun to have him along, riding next to her through the avenues lined with blooming chestnut trees, looking proud and dashing on his black stallion while she will be reclining on silk cushions and dazzling all onlookers with her stunning new feather hat. . . .

Hope revives in Octavian as he hears the Marschallin mention a messenger; all she invites him to is a ride through the Prater, but even so he accepts eagerly, because the mere prospect of seeing her again is bliss. He will be riding by the side of her carriage, and she will be gazing up at him with that tender passion he knows so well.

He is about to kiss her hand and then go on from there to kiss her arm, but a defensive gesture on her part restrains him.

"Now be a good boy," she says lightly, as though addressing a child, "and do as you're told."

All he can do is click his heels, bow, and leave; any further plea would be distinctly undignified. "At your orders, Bichette," he snaps, rushing out.

The Marschallin did want him to leave; but now that he is gone, her hand, still raised to emphasize her request, slowly sinks to her side. The hand feels a void, and the eyes, raised in reproach a moment before, now see only the emptiness of the cold, large room. That silly, fickle heart of hers. She could at least have sent him off with a warm, gentle kiss instead of showing exasperation. She sent him away without at least one more kiss; why did she rob herself of that sweet moment? Are there going to be that many more of them? Is she still so rich that she can afford to waste happiness? Abruptly she calls for the servants and orders them to hurry after the Count and bring him back.

But the servants return empty-handed; the Count had rushed out so fast and ridden off in such haste, never once looking back, that all their shouting after him was in vain.

The Marschallin, leaning against the dressing table, makes an effort to regain her composure; she does not want the servants to perceive her inner turmoil. Outwardly calm, she rings for her little Moor, hands him the red case with the silver rose, and orders him to deliver it to Count Octavian.

As he prances off, a sudden premonition of disaster takes hold of her; she feels as though she were sending her happiness away with the silver rose. She is about to recall the Moor, but the door closing on him brings her back to her senses. A case of nerves, she decides; she is no longer young enough to bear up under the strain of passion. She had better forget her silly premonitions; what she needs is a rest.

Slowly dragging her feet, she walks over to the dressing table and seats herself in utter exhaustion. As she glances up, unwitting, she meets in her mirror the eyes of an aging woman whose wilted features presage the end. Quickly she picks up the hand mirror and carefully examines the crow's-feet around her eyes. The mirror drops from her hand, and she wipes its surface as though to erase the image; then her head droops and she is about to let herself go, break out in sobs, surrender to the luxury of despair. Tears would do her good. On the other hand, she remembers her earlier monologue; one has to take things as they come, take and hold happiness with a light heart and a light touch, and when the time comes, let go. . . . A smile of gentle resignation flashes around her lips, and she now bows her head, not as a woman crushed, but as one reconciled to the inevitable.

The curtain comes down very slowly upon the Marschallin seated in the center of the stage, a lone but gallant figure, tired and pensive, gently serene.

I cannot conclude this discussion of the first act without mentioning an episode of which I am ashamed to this day, though it happened in 1938 in London. Covent Garden seemed the same as ever, a friendly and familiar place; but all the roles in *Der Rosenkavalier* had been reassigned, with only myself as the Marschallin representing the Old Guard. Octavian was sung by Tiana Lemnitz, an excellent and exceedingly ambitious young singer. The entire cast had come from Berlin so that I, an unequivocal and staunch opponent of the Nazi regime, felt surrounded by enemies, with only Sir Thomas Beecham, the conductor, as my friend.

On the day of the performance, moreover, I had received bad news. My husband had fallen ill with tuberculosis, the dread disease that was to kill him within a year, and the children of his first marriage, being half-Jewish, were in acute danger now that Vienna had been taken over by the Nazis.

This convergence of fear and suspicion must have brought about a hysterical paralysis of the vocal cords. During the first act I felt my voice gradually giving out. Finally I stood there absolutely mute, unable to control myself. I left the stage, and the curtain was lowered, whereupon for the first and last time in my life I fainted. At least I think I must have fainted, for I do not remember anything until I found myself sitting in my dressing room with a doctor in attendance. He diagnosed a hysterical paralysis of the vocal cords and predicted a quick and spontaneous recovery. I could not, of course, go on that night, and I do not recall who took my place; the entire episode is blurred even in memory.

I still feel very strongly, however, that I should have overcome my fear. I broke the first commandment of show business—the show must go on—and never have quite been able to forgive myself for this failure. Nothing should have been allowed to stand in the way of my fulfilling my duties and obligations. By plunging into the role I should have made myself forget all thoughts of personal suffering. I failed, and the nagging memory of that failure, pursuing me through the years, has been my punishment.

Incidentally, Sir Thomas made sure that even that terrible episode ended on a mildly humorous note. He came to see me in my dressing room, and, when on emerging he found himself surrounded by a glum and worried crowd, he issued a bulletin on the spot. "No grounds for concern," he said, smiling, and with a mischievous twinkle in his eyes. "Madame is being attended to by a very handsome young doctor. She'll recover presently, I'm sure."

In the second act the Marschallin does not appear onstage at all, but for the singer this apparent respite is in fact more taxing than uninterrupted singing. The inner tension is left to relax, the concentrated unity of mood is broken, and the return onstage always involves an inner struggle. In Vienna my dressing room always was transformed into a meeting place rather resembling the Marschallin's own antechamber, with a constant stream of visitors, most of them members of the cast who also happened to be free at the moment. Whenever the stage manager wanted to round up his actors, he invariably used to come to my room rather than go to that of the person he was looking for; experience had taught him to look there for whomever he sought. There would be Bella Paalen as Annina, convincingly Italian with her black hair and classic Roman features; Alfred Muzzarelli, called "Muzzi" for short, who sang the Notary and pleasantly whiled away his free periods chatting and chuckling with me, and many others, all of them very helpful to both my voice and my mood. Muzzi had a habit of switching voice teachers constantly and was obsessed by hankerings for absolute perfection. His deep bass voice stubbornly refused to master the soft head tone he dreamed of, a fact that cost him much heartache; but time and again he would find "the right teacher at last," with a new and guaranteed way of mastering the head tone.

After the war, when at last communication with Vienna was resumed, I received among many others a letter from Muzzi, in his own characteristic vein, and I really did not know whether to laugh or cry. Along with all the others, he had suffered a great deal, had been caught in the Opera during an air raid and had managed at the last moment to escape from the burning building. The loss of the Opera was a blow to him, as it was to all Viennese; even people not connected with it in any way, who loved it as a monument of musical culture, were standing out in the street, tears streaming down their faces as they watched the burning building. Every Viennese felt it as a personal loss.

How much more keenly, then, must the loss have been felt by those who regarded the Opera as their own true home. In his letter, Muzzi movingly described the destruction of the beautiful building and what it meant to him personally. But in the very next passage he emerged once again as his former self —at long last, he wrote, he had mastered that blessed head tone, he could do it to perfection, and now no one in the world could teach him anything about technique. I replied at once to tell him how happy I had been to find at least one point of reference unchanged in this turbulent world of ours; Europe lay in ashes, the atom bomb threatened universal doom —but there was Muzzi raving about his head tone, writing about it in his very first letter after all he had been through. And I really do think it charming, indicative of the degree to which we artists tend to live in a world of our own. Material existence seems almost unimportant; we have our own very special problems, real enough, no matter how childish they may appear to outsiders. Muzzi, as it happens, was an extraordinarily intelligent human being, with a lively sense of humor and interests ranging far beyond his profession. Still, his profession meant a great deal more to him than merely a way of making a living, and, though his career was unfortunately never to be particularly brilliant, he loved it with all his heart and soul, no matter how much he would gripe and curse about it. His life's goal was to sing ever better, and he continued to persist in it long after he must have realized that fame would elude him forever. That is how one must love singing in order to become a true artist. Muzzi was a man who never reached the top, who knew that he never would get there, and who yet was incurably addicted to the theater.

He died some years ago, and Vienna without him will never again be quite the same to me.

Act Two

The second-act curtain rises on the ornate reception hall in the mansion of wealthy Herr von Faninal, who refers to this

brand-new house as his "town palace." The entire household
is in an uproar; Sophie, the daughter just graduated from convent school, has been betrothed to a so-called nobleman whose
arrival is expected at any moment. Her father had shown
indecent hurry to marry her off to someone of the "proper"
class, meaning the top-level aristocracy from which his origins thus far have barred him despite his immense wealth.
Sophie's convent undoubtedly must have been Sacre-Coeur;
that is where the daughters of socially prominent Viennese
families usually were sent for the proper kind of education,
which of course excluded any and all knowledge of the facts
of life as lived in the world beyond the convent walls. Elisabeth Schumann as Sophie to a marked degree possessed the
shy loveliness of a terribly young and vulnerably innocent
creature roused to struggle for the first time in her life by the
insulting brutality of her fiancé, Baron Ochs.

At the beginning of the second act, however, she still is
dreamily eager and expectant, waiting for the divine husband
that her father has promised her. Her father must know that
she can be happy only with someone truly good and noble,
and when in a pompous tone of voice he announces her impending betrothal, she gratefully kisses his hand.

Faninal has hired an experienced Majordomo who, realizing
that his master's manners are badly in need of improvement,
has become teacher and arbiter in matters of etiquette. He now
informs Faninal that the rules preclude the father's presence
at the arrival of the Rose-Bearer, and he clearly is upset at
Faninal's unctuous speeches which keep him lingering on long
past the point of decency. The Majordomo takes his job very
seriously, and part of it consists of making sure that everything moves like clockwork and that no one can find cause
for criticizing any aspect of the ceremonial.

Finally the master yields and leaves Sophie alone with the
governess, Marianne Leitmetzerin. Sophie tries to pray, as she

was taught at Sacre-Coeur, but it is impossible to listen to the governess's exciting account of what is going on downstairs in the street while at the same time seeking peace and serenity in prayer. The actual arrival of the Rose-Bearer is witnessed by both women as well as by the entire audience, with the music dramatically and sweepingly intensifying the stage effects and involving the audience in the anticipation felt by Sophie as she looks forward to this most important moment in her young life.

Musically the arrival of Octavian is framed in the sort of glamour that only Richard Strauss was able to create; the truly magnificent duet between Sophie and Octavian contains all the splendor of youth and all the beauty embodied by these two human beings.

And the inevitable happens, as it must—Octavian immediately and desperately falls in love with the girl.

After the sophisticated subtlety of the Marschallin, he is instinctively overreceptive to the attraction of innocence untouched and unsullied. The girl is still half a child, and her childish patter is largely nonsense; but he is surfeited with knowledgeable adult conversation, delighted to be listening to Sophie's gibberish, happy not to be "the boy" for once, but rather a man to whom this girl is looking up. Sophie's governess intently follows the conversation and reacts to each sentence uttered by her protégée, but she should always remain in the background and never divert attention to herself by excessive participation. A minor sort of comic exchange actually takes place between her and Sophie; at first Sophie anxiously looks to her for help, not knowing what to say to the handsome young Count, and when in all innocence she drops the name Quinquin, the governess is petrified. Vienna is a city of gossip and if one of her servants had even heard by chance the Marschallin call Octavian Quinquin it would soon be common knowledge, withheld only from her husband, since the Viennese always had great understanding for illicit affairs.

Octavian is embarrassed in turn, but at the same time utterly charmed by Sophie's childlike innocence. This is different from his experience with the oversophisticated Marschallin—an affair that was to last through all eternity and is about to come to an end because his happiness lies in Sophie's lovely eyes.

The arrival of Baron Ochs understandably upsets Sophie who is horrified by this vile, vulgar creature meant to be her fiancé. He behaves with more than his customary impertinence, and Octavian repeatedly reaches for his sword, but time and again stops himself; he is, after all, a guest in this house. Baron Ochs immediately notices the resemblance between Octavian and the pretty chambermaid and is sufficiently tactless to remark on it, proving how accurately the Marschallin had foreseen the situation and how brilliantly her scheme had prevented a possible catastrophe.

Baron Ochs is not only unsuspecting; he is, in fact, in a downright jovial mood. Sophie pleases him very much. He has looked her over as if she were a horse and has pronounced himself satisfied with his buy. The future father-in-law, who has joined the group, is most obsequious and, along with all other members of the household, laughs uproariously at everyone of the Baron's vulgar jokes. In fact everyone, with the obvious exception of Sophie and Octavian, seems thoroughly delighted with the "noble Fiancé" and poor little Sophie meets with neither sympathy nor understanding when in despair she seeks protection from her father against the brutally direct advances made by her suitor. Octavian, on the other hand, is almost beside himself with rage. Seething, he time and again battles the urge to put an end to this villainous game; he still wants to adhere to the code of behavior imposed upon him as guest of the house. But his heart beats in uncontrolled fury against the Baron and with love for this pretty child, whom he longs to protect and to rescue from the horrible fate of becoming the prey of so base an intrigue.

The Baron finally leaves the room to devote himself to what he considers the most important business at hand, drawing up the marriage contract. Sophie and Octavian thus are left alone, and Octavian uses the opportunity to promise the girl his help, to declare his love, and to ask for her hand in marriage. Their ecstatic duet is interrupted by the Italian couple, hired by the Baron to spy on his future wife in the guise of servants. Promptly keeping their part of the bargain, they summon the Baron and inform him that they caught Sophie and Octavian in a compromising situation.

A violent quarrel now ensues between Ochs and Octavian, who demands that the Baron reconsider his marital plans in view of the fact that his intended bride despises him. Ochs is inclined to regard the whole matter as rather funny; he sneers at Octavian and quite obviously does not have the slightest intention of giving up the Faninal fortune and the heiress that goes with it. On the contrary: he is determined to make her live up to her father's promise and put her signature to the marriage contract. So provocative is his behavior that in the end Octavian simply cannot contain himself any longer; drawing his sword, he slightly scratches the Baron's arm in a brief duel. The Baron's most undignified screams bring the whole household running. Herr Faninal, outraged at Octavian's behavior, bars his house to him thenceforth and forevermore and threatens to put his daughter away in a cloister for the rest of her life unless she marries the Baron. In the midst of the general uproar, Octavian quietly slips out, but on the way is accosted by the two Italians, who have shrewdly decided that it would be to their advantage to switch sides and bank on Octavian's generosity rather than on the obviously stingy and shabby Baron Ochs. Octavian, barely interested at first, suddenly has an inspiration and asks them to come with him.

Baron Ochs in the meantime loudly laments his misfortune, rails at the "miserable young whippersnapper," but also is compelled, rather against his will, to laugh at the boy's colossal nerve. The Baron used to be young, too, once upon a time. He finds Sophie rather amusing also; he liked her spunky show of resistance. He always has wanted his girls that way; breaking their resistance is part of the fun. Sipping his wine happily and against explicit doctor's orders, he is contemplating his rosy future with undiminished satisfaction when the door opens and Annina, the Italian girl, hands him a letter.

The Marschallin has imbued Octavian with a taste for subtle intrigue, and in his alter ego of "Mariandl, the pretty chambermaid," he has sent the Baron a note suggesting a tryst. His ultimate purpose is to compromise the Baron to the point at which even Sophie's father will recoil from such a son-in-law.

The Baron in his simpleminded eagerness swallows the bait, and the act closes upon his executing a tipsy waltz, triumphantly believing that now at last he has everything a man could possibly desire—a wealthy heiress, a fortune, and a pretty chambermaid mistress.

And in my mind's eye I can still see the curtain going down upon Richard Mayr's cunning face, and I can still hear his tipsy voice singing "With me no night is going to be long enough for you. . . ."

Act Three

The third act takes place in the disreputable tavern chosen by the Baron for his meeting with the presumptive chambermaid. An elaborate plot has been worked out by Octavian, and the act opens on what, in a manner of speaking, is a full dress rehearsal. Valzacchi, the Italian, has done a good job; his men are hidden everywhere, and at a sign from him they will come streaming out and frighten the Baron into betraying himself. Annina is to come in disguised as a widow, followed by a slew of children who will accuse the Baron not only of being their father but also of having deserted their poor mother. Everything is designed to create the utmost confusion.

Utmost confusion is indeed what characterizes the first half of the third act, which in a sense is "overplayed." But Hofmannsthal was trying to depict the somewhat childish pleasure people in those days used to take in such exaggerated comedies.

Octavian, already in his chambermaid disguise, makes all the actors run through a complete rehearsal and, expressing his satisfaction, in the end rewards Valzacchi's cunning with a generous purse. He thereupon briefly disappears, to re-enter moments later as a shy little kitten being led by Baron Ochs.

There follows a very funny scene in which Octavian makes believe he is getting drunker by the minute, with much maudlin sobbing and sighing. The Baron, however, wanting action, proceeds to make ever more daring advances, until suddenly he notices the somber and savage-looking ruffians slinking and lurking all about him, uncanny faces that he tries to ignore by taking a few quick drinks. But the faces will not be ignored, and so finally, quite fitting into Octavian's scheme, the Baron's terror gets the better of him. Opening the window, he screams for help, whereupon the so-called widow appears and, with her brood of children, chases him around the room. Mobs from everywhere seem to be converging on the Baron, who has long since lost interest in his tryst and wants nothing so much as to get away as fast and as far as possible.

In the meantime Valzacchi, as directed by Octavian, has sent for Sophie's father, whom Octavian wants to witness this evidence of immorality.

Instead, in response to all the excitement, the morals squad arrives, a trifle too soon to suit Octavian's purpose. He would have much preferred to have them wait until after old Faninal's appearance; for if the police were to settle matters before the father's arrival, the impact would certainly be nowhere near as effective as the version planned by Octavian.

Seeing the police officer, the Baron heaves a sigh of relief. He is, after all, a well-known personality, a member of the aristocracy, and the mere mention of his name will so impress the police officer that he not only will have this bandits' nest cleaned out at once but also will afford the Baron a second chance to conquer the charming chambermaid.

As it turns out, Baron Ochs is sadly mistaken. The police officer curtly points out that anybody can call himself Baron von Lerchenau and that he would take nobody's word for it without either witnesses or other identification. Nothing simpler than that, replies Baron Ochs, calling upon both Valzacchi and the Innkeeper to identify him. But both men refuse. They suddenly are not at all certain. "The gentleman may well be a baron, and then again he may not," says Valzacchi, while the Innkeeper simply follows Octavian's orders by shrugging his shoulders and muttering something to the effect that he "knows nothing."

Leopold, the Baron's valet and illegitimate son, is terribly worried about the dangerous situation into which his father and master has worked himself and is racking his brains for some way of helping him when suddenly he conceives the glorious idea of getting in touch with the Marschallin. Impulsively acting on it, he runs off at once. This minor scene, so very essential to an understanding of the whole situation, as a rule passes completely unnoticed by the audience, though without it the Marschallin's appearance in this shabby, disreputable hotel seems incomprehensible.

Octavian, trying to draw the police officer's attention to himself, now starts to whimper and complain, running in feigned confusion toward the curtained-off bed, showing it to the officer and explaining in some detail the true purpose of the Baron's visit to this den of iniquity. The Baron, cornered, hastily explains that the young lady is his intended wife, Fräulein Faninal. Concerned solely with extricating himself from a somewhat embarrassing situation, he is not the least bit hesitant about compromising Sophie and ruining her reputation.

At that precise moment, Faninal himself enters the room, providing a most unpleasant surprise. Informed by the police officer of the Baron's explanation, Faninal first rails at the officer for daring to cast suspicion on his innocent daughter, waiting downstairs in his carriage, and thereupon collapses in a dead faint, to be carried into the adjoining room and attended to by Sophie and by all his servants.

The Baron, left face to face with the police officer, quickly regains his composure. "I'll pay," he boldly suggests, "I'll leave, I'll take her home." But the police officer, not that easily put off, has determined to go on with the interrogation when Octavian approaches and, in a quick, whispered confession, avows the truth. The officer is wildly amused to discover that the whole thing is a hoax, and he watches with unrepressed glee as the young Count changes clothes behind a screen.

The all-out confusion is compounded abruptly by the arrival of the Innkeeper, all out of breath with excitement and announcing Her Ducal Highness, the Duchess Marschallin.

Leopold, the Baron's dim-witted servant-son, had delivered himself of a garbled account from which the Marschallin, by dint of sheer perspicacity, finally gathered that his father and master had been caught in a most compromising situation while trysting with "Chambermaid Mariandl" and that the morals squad is about to haul him off to jail.

What has shocked the Marschallin is Octavian's brazen determination to go on with the masquerade and carry it beyond a mere joke. What is his game? She got ready at once and had herself driven to this disreputable tavern, where under normal circumstances she would never have set foot, not the least bit interested in helping the Baron, but intent only on finding out what Octavian is up to.

Swiftly she walks into the tavern, and her entrance is musically one of the most beautiful highlights of the opera. Out of the chaos and confusion of the preceding scene emerges a broad, flowing theme that enfolds the Marschallin like a river of beauty. Frantic disorder is transfigured into noble sound, and the Marschallin now becomes the center of attention as she casts indignant glances all about her, seemingly enraged at the effrontery of those who have dared to lure her into this hellhole of depravity, though the decision to come had been entirely her own. But she never before has been in a place like this one, and now, with an expression of truly Olympian superiority, she takes the center of the stage. The Baron, stupid enough to assume that she has come solely for his sake, is quick to express his gratitude for this tangible evidence of her friendship and esteem, while Octavian, still dressing behind the screen, peers across it at the Marschallin with apprehensive surprise, greatly embarrassed at this turn of events. The Marschallin, in turn, has not yet seen him, and she stands motionless, her back half turned toward the Baron while the police officer steps up to greet and salute her. Thanking the officer in a tone of easy and amiable condescension, the Marschallin eyes him more closely. His face seems familiar, and suddenly she realizes that the man used to be one of her husband's aides. She had noticed him at the time because he was a smart and good-looking young man, and the Marschallin always has had an eye for good-looking young men. Raising her lorgnette for a closer look at him, she quickly confirms her impression by a few questions and finally rewards the man with one of her own very special smiles.

The Baron, in the meantime, desperately tries to signal to

Octavian, his greatest worry at the moment being to keep the pseudo-maid from showing herself before the Marschallin. The latter, however, notices his frantic efforts and turns at the very instant when Octavian, now in his own clothes, emerges from behind the screen. Their eyes meet, and the Marschallin, aware of his helpless embarrassment, is immediately convinced that he continued the masquerade for the sake of a girl and that she has lost him to another. "Today, tomorrow, or the day after . . ."

This, then, is the day.

The Marschallin is a woman of class, an aristocrat from head to toe. Her quietly questioning glance meets Octavian's plainly troubled one. "This isn't quite the way it was planned," the boy stammers. They had planned, of course, to meet in the Prater and to ride side by side through the glorious park, and a meeting here, in this tavern, was about the last thing either of them had expected.

Entering now by the right-hand door is Sophie, still unaware of the Marschallin, who is hidden by the Baron's squat figure. The young girl has regained all her composure, and nothing could have pleased her more than the terrible mess by which the Baron now has compromised himself so completely. As yet she has no idea that the trap was both baited and sprung by Octavian, but she does know that her father is outraged by the Baron's behavior and that the dreaded wedding has been avoided. Sophie, deriving understandable comfort and satisfaction from being able to tell the obnoxious Baron exactly what she thinks of him, has come to deliver her father's message; and the words "My father wants me to tell you . . ." with which she addresses her ex-fiancé are sung with lively contempt.

Sophie's arrival greatly troubles and embarrasses the Baron, who would have given much to avoid having the Marschallin learn all the sordid details of his sad defeat. He therefore tries to get rid of the girl as fast as possible by shoving her out of sight.

The Marschallin, however, at the sound of the girl's voice has turned around at once, and now, to the extent this is possible despite the Baron's frantic attempts, she carefully scrutinizes Sophie through her lorgnette. Octavian, still in the throes of his deadly embarrassment, vainly tries to explain what the Marschallin has grasped within the fraction of an instant; with a friendly smile she therefore puts an end to his painful verbal contortions. "Methinks you're much impressed, Rofrano. I can imagine who she is. And I must say, I find her charming."

All the Marschallin's intentions, her firm resolve to accept the inevitable and give up Octavian with grace and friendly resignation, here find their fulfillment. Locking up her pain and trouble within herself, she from the very first moment hits upon the exact tone in which to conclude an affair that had meant a great deal to her. Her calling him "Rofrano" rather than "Quinquin" already defines the distance between them. From now on she is going to be the "Marschallin," as far as he is concerned. She cannot, however, quite suppress a trace of irony as she contemplates the young lady for whose sake Octavian is deserting her—charming, certainly, a delightful little girl, but other than that the Marschallin can see nothing in this still rather childlike creature. Her sole virtues are youth and spiritual innocence, two attributes the Marschallin herself lost long before and does not hold in unduly high esteem.

Sophie still has not noticed the Marschallin. In her nimble-witted Viennese way she gives the Baron a tongue-lashing, brashly candid and with true Viennese pertness to which the Marschallin listens with delight, gratified that at long last this despicable cousin of hers is caught in a trap from which he cannot wiggle free, and that the tragedy of his marrying this girl has been averted. She herself, of course, had been badly bruised in the process, but no one ever will know. Accustomed to command, to take charge, she now rises to the occasion by intervening abruptly and with majestic serenity. Touching the Baron's shoulder lightly with her fan, she stops his furious outburst at Sophie and curtly orders him to get out. Aghast at this unexpected lack of class solidarity, the Baron wonders aloud how a lady like the Marschallin can take the part of a member of the lower class. But the Marschallin tauntingly urges him to watch out for his dignity. "Take whatever dignity you have left, and get out." Measuring him with a disdainful glance from head to toe, she publicly informs the Baron that his now somewhat shaky position as a member of the nobility hinges solely upon his knowing how to grin and bear it. Then, turning to the police officer, she requests that no one be troubled any further in this affair, because she does not want to see Octavian involved in this murky business. Nor, for that matter, does she herself want to be implicated in any manner whatsoever. The police officer obediently takes off, and the Marschallin next devotes herself to Sophie, who greets her with a deep curtsy. But the Baron, contrary to all expectations, stubbornly insists that he will not under any circumstances give up his erstwhile fiancée.

From the Marschallin's point of view matters could scarcely be worse than they are. Her elaborate scheme designed to befuddle the Baron and conceal her affair with Octavian has obviously misfired; Octavian may have done a noble deed for Sophie, but he certainly has got the Marschallin into a heap of trouble. Sooner or later the Baron is bound to recount the whole adventure to his cronies, including the story of the Marschallin's chambermaid who willingly dated him and willingly would have done more than that if it had not been for the untimely arrival of the morals squad. And when that story reaches the ears of her husband, as it is bound to sooner or later, he inevitably will want to see this famous chambermaid—so all her clever plans have come to naught.

With lightning speed she now decides upon a complete reversal of strategy. By letting the Baron in on her secret and making him an accomplice of sorts, she may be able to buy his silence; would he ever on his own confess to his cronies that he made a fool of himself and tried to seduce a maid that turned out to be a man?

The Marschallin makes up her mind to take a chance, and with an imperious gesture urges Octavian to step forward and make the Baron come to his senses. The Baron recoils in utter amazement, then gives Octavian a dagger look of bitter sarcasm. "I've had it," he says. "The sight of this face makes me sick. He's a man, all right."

The Marschallin, regaining her composure, now attempts to smooth things over to some extent by explaining that the whole situation was a sort of Viennese masquerade. With a look of lofty condescension which instantly raises the walls between her and the Baron, she haughtily informs him that otherwise she most certainly would not have idly stood by while he proceeded to debauch her chambermaid. Withdrawn, the Marschallin says, without looking at Octavian but nevertheless addressing him, that she has had enough of men. "Of men in general. Of all men."

The Baron, meanwhile, has bounced back and reverted to his own impertinent self. The full significance of what the Marschallin referred to as a Viennese masquerade is beginning to dawn on him, and with it the realization that he now holds a powerful weapon against her. With his customary crude candor he proceeds to make this obvious at once, exclaiming that Octavian's presence in the Marschallin's bedroom certainly would seem to create some delicate problems.

The Marschallin appears profoundly shaken, for with all her contempt for the Baron she nonetheless has failed to appreciate the full extent of his colossal impudence and vulgarity. She certainly never would have believed him capable of coming out in public with an announcement that he understood what it would have been his duty as a gentleman not to understand. With a disdainful gesture she restrains Octavian who is about to draw his sword. No, she needs no protector; she is very well able to take care of herself in dealing with creatures of the Baron's ilk. Then, her seething indignation encased in a mask of perfunctory amiability, in a level tone of indifference she informs Baron Ochs that she always had thought of him as a gentleman. "And if you are a gentleman," she continues, "you'll think *nothing*. Nothing at all. This is what I *expect* of you . . ." The word *expect* is emphasized in the manner of both a threat and an absolute order, and the Baron instantly senses the imperative nature of her command. Pulling himself together, he attempts with feigned casualness to pretend to a vestige of social graces; somehow the Marschallin's appeal to his gallantry flatters his ego. Marvelous woman. Knows that she can count on him, a gentleman of the old school. Would never dream of uttering threats against him, the Baron Ochs von Lerchenau. Gets her way instead by a mere delicate hint—though it takes a gentleman such as he to understand.

Tensely the Marschallin waits for his answer. Then, realizing that the uncouth creature has been tamed, she disgustedly walks toward the right side of the stage, because now the Baron, instead of quietly disappearing, gives noisy and voluble expression to his immense joy at having become privy to so piquant a secret.

The Baron, in fact, is far from ready to leave. Greed and cunning make him want to cash in on his discovery, and veiled blackmail seems opportune. He already has figured out that by his silence he is rendering the Marschallin a great service; it is only right, then, for her in turn to do him a favor, such as putting in a good word on his behalf with Sophie's father. Boldly, therefore, he steps over to the door, about to summon Faninal into the Marschallin's presence, fully expecting her to restore him to his former glory as a highly eligible son-in-law.

But at long last the Marschallin loses her patience. The monstrous brutality of his behavior forces her to drop the mask of amiability to which thus far she has clung, and she begins to understand that there is only one way of dealing with this vulgar loudmouth. Erect, hand pointing to the door, she orders him to leave: "Get out." In an unrestrained outburst of temper she lets him know in unmistakable terms that the game is up, that he is through, and that he had better forget about the marriage and everything that goes with it.

In the end Baron Ochs surrenders meekly, bowing to the stronger will, mechanically echoing her words like a child whipped into obedience at last.

Sophie, who had been watching this entire scene, is utterly baffled by it and has not the faintest notion what it is all about. She is at a loss to explain Octavian's presence. Nor can she understand the relationship between him, the Baron, and the Marschallin. But she does begin to suspect that something is amiss and that between Octavian and the Marschallin there is some hidden link, the true nature of which she can only guess at. A vague fear chills her heart; has she lost Octavian? And if so, to whom? According to the Marschallin, marriage is now out of the question—but which marriage? Marriage to the monster Baron, or the other one that she, Sophie, secretly has been dreaming about? Quietly, with trembling lips, she repeats the Marschallin's final *"It's all finished."*

The Marschallin, hearing her own words echoed by the girl, is struck by their double meaning. Yes, it is all finished; she has lost Octavian. Slowly she turns to the young Count, and with a sad long look takes leave of him. "So that's it," she quietly says, more or less to herself.

Octavian, pale and silent, stands in the center of the stage.

He feels guilty and would like to kneel before the Marschallin, to ask for her blessing and forgiveness. But he feels himself driven by an irresistible compulsion, and his passion for the mature woman that mere hours ago seemed destined to last forever is now at most the pale shadow of a memory. His heart belongs to Sophie, and the Marschallin once again has been proved right—he is leaving her for another.

The extras hired by Octavian for his plot against the Baron now start crowding into the room to present their bills to none other than Baron Ochs and to press for immediate payment, because Octavian, to top off his joke, has charged all expenses against the victim.

The Marschallin crosses to the right side of the stage, and Octavian, seeing that she is anxious to be gone, offers her a chair. Though unwilling to linger, she does stop near the window.

This is a dark moment in her life. She has done what had to be done, has saved the entire situation without obtaining anything in return. A lonely figure, she stands by the window, aware that Octavian's heart is far away, though his eyes seek hers with an anxious, questioning look. And ahead lies the hardest task yet; she herself must bring the young couple together. It is far from easy to do this gracefully without time for inner preparation, to be plunged abruptly from the heights of a glorious love affair into the bleak abyss of loneliness.

And after all it would seem irrelevant whether or not the Marschallin loves young Octavian so passionately that she never will forget him. Perhaps he is merely another affair, one out of many, rather than the "great love" of her life; personally I do not believe the Marschallin to be the sort of woman who will go on mourning her lost love forever, and resign herself henceforth to a life of ascetic loneliness. She is far too much a child of her time, a temperamental creature in the best years of life, worldly-wise and eager for adventure.

But these considerations in no way detract from the tragedy as she experiences it at the moment. A lover always will believe in the immutable permanence of her feelings, and the end of every love affair is always a small death. Something of transcendent beauty is at this instant dying in the Marschallin, and she buries it in her soul with the feeling that thenceforth she will be all alone in the world.

Here the audience must be able to divine the inner struggle that is rending the Marschallin. She should not just be standing there by the window, but rather must impress upon the onlooker the feeling that this, as far as she is concerned, is the hour of decision.

Slowly regaining her composure, she resignedly turns back toward the stage, paying no attention to Octavian and watching instead with contemptuous indifference the noisy gang of servants. Finally the two Italians leave the stage along with Baron Ochs, and the Marschallin is left alone with Sophie and Octavian.

Sophie is terribly upset. She sees Octavian staying close to the Marschallin as though chained to her by invisible chains, watching her every move and paying no attention to anyone else. He seems to have forgotten all about Sophie. That lady over there, whose glamour and regal splendor make Sophie feel small and insignificant, appears to be holding Octavian's fate in the palm of her hand, and the young girl simply does not know what to make of it all.

Octavian, in turn, is embarrassed to death. He feels obliged to ask the Marschallin's forgiveness, but does not know how to go about it, and his unseemly stammer only makes matters worse by exasperating the Marschallin, who would like to get the whole business over with as quickly as possible, to have Octavian join Sophie and go where he belongs. "Go quickly," she therefore tells him, with somewhat acid emphasis. "Follow your heart's desire."

Octavian would be only too happy to do so, but he is tormented by guilt, knowing how profoundly he has hurt the Marschallin. He stands trapped between the two women, unable to come to terms with himself and to decide on the right thing to do. The Marschallin once more makes up his mind for him. "Show you are a man," she hisses, furiously. "Go to her!"

At this he leaves her side and goes over to Sophie. But now the girl rejects him and stands there, truculent, replying to his fervent pleas with flippant irony. She is no baby, either, she informs him. She is a bright young thing from Vienna, and no one can do this to her and get away with it. Here she had thought that he loved her—and now what? She is ashamed to look at the Marschallin and does not even know why, and Octavian is not much help at all. No help, in fact.

The Marschallin listens to their quarrel and senses the underlying tension; and as Octavian uses the very words he had whispered into her ear so often while making love—"I swear you are my soul and happiness"—she is badly shaken. Rising, she quietly repeats what she has told herself so many times already: "Today, tomorrow, or the day after . . ." And while Octavian utters promises of love eternal to Sophie, the Marschallin realizes that she is merely going through what every woman must go through at least once in a lifetime—the torments of resignation.

At the end of the brief trio, she gently turns toward Octavian. Sophie, misunderstanding the gesture, believes that he is being summoned.

A moment's confusion.

Calmly the Marschallin bides her time. She does not want to make things too easy for Octavian either. Let him prove himself a man of the world, able to handle this sort of predicament. But he, alas, stands helpless between the two women, anxiously trying to keep Sophie from walking off while at the same time groping for words to explain his feelings to the Marschallin. Sophie, mortally embarrassed, wants to get away as fast as possible, and Octavian's desperate efforts to hold her back elicit a sad smile from the Marschallin. So this is how far they already have drifted apart, she thinks; already he is afraid to be alone in a room with her. He certainly has not come to know her very well if he thinks that she is about to assail him with a flood of tears and reproaches.

Realizing reluctantly that she herself will have to take whatever action is required, the Marschallin turns to Sophie. Benevolently watching the girl's confusion as reflected in the pretty young face, she inquires if Octavian really means that much to her already. "I don't know what your Highness is trying to tell me," is about all that Sophie can bring herself to utter when the Marschallin, lightly touching the girl's cheek with her fan, flashes a smile tinged with a trace of irony. "The pallor of your face is enough of an answer," she says, whereupon Sophie splutteringly hastens to express her gratitude to the Marschallin and to explain the whole series of predicaments with a childish impetuosity that sharpens the edge of sarcasm in the Marschallin's smile.

How, she wonders, was it possible for Octavian to fall head over heels in love with this utterly commonplace child? A woman probably never can really appreciate a rival's true worth and attraction, and the Marschallin here sees only a rather pretty young girl chattering away at a great rate, spouting a great deal of nonsense, and looking, at best, cute. Hiding her animosity, she interrupts Sophie with a gentle gesture. "Don't talk so much. You don't have to. You're pretty enough."

"Pretty enough" is precisely her impression. A pretty face, and that, apparently, was all it took to kindle Octavian's infatuation.

She now decides to take the entire situation into her generous and capable hands, offering to inform Sophie's father that young Count Octavian will make a far more eligible son-in-law than the disreputable Baron von Lerchenau. Faninal is bound to take her word for it. Furthermore, she will offer him her own carriage and extend an invitation to her palace, all of which will unquestionably make the eager Faninal dissolve in sheer bliss.

Sophie, overwhelmed by so much kindness, curtsies deeply. "Your Highness," she stammers, "is kindness in person." The Marschallin, patting Sophie under the chin, lifts up the girl's face and gives her a tender smile. "As to that pallor, my child," she says, "methinks that my cousin over there has the supreme remedy."

Her emotions now threaten to get the better of her, and it costs her a real effort to utter this last phrase, for the remedy that her "cousin" has in store for Sophie, his kisses and caresses, are the very things she herself will have to do without from now on.

Octavian, profoundly moved, approaches her shyly. "Marie Theres'," he says, "I simply can't tell you how truly good and great you are. I just simply don't know . . ." He stops.

The Marschallin stands completely motionless. She wants to hear nothing more, wants to be left alone. Toneless, teeth clenched, she answers: "I don't know, either. I don't know anything."

Octavian is utterly lost for a moment, and his whispered "Marie Theres' " is at once a plea, a vow, and a question. So overwhelmed is he by the great Marie Theres', by her warmth and generosity, that I have always felt his destiny to be entirely in her hands. I believe that if at that moment she had turned to him and asked him not to leave her, he would have obeyed. But the Marschallin is both greater and wiser than that; she turns to him only to bid him adieu.

The divine trio that follows is the grand climax of the

beautiful opera, with three voices fusing in harmonious purity of ineffable depth.

Sophie senses that what the Marschallin is about to pass on to her is her own happiness; it is as though she were receiving Octavian from the hands of this woman as a gift for life, and yet it also seems as though the Marschallin had taken something from Octavian that Sophie never can hope to possess.

Octavian feels that destiny has taken charge of him. He would like nothing so much as to ask the Marschallin's advice, yet even he now realizes that she is the last person in the world to whom he can turn for help in this matter. Did he do wrong? He is merely obeying a force stronger than himself.

The Marschallin reminds herself that she swore to love him "in the right manner"—meaning that she would let go of him and be able even to like the woman for whose sake he left her. All this may seem rather implausible to someone who has not been through it, but she knows it to be the truth. Once upon a time Octavian was part of her; now he stands over there, he belongs to a stranger, and he will be happy with that stranger to the extent to which a man ever can be happy with a woman.

The Marschallin now feels superfluous, and with a long last glance at the two youngsters, who have eyes only for each other, she mutters a blessing and leaves the room.

Octavian and Sophie fail to notice the Marschallin's departure. They fall into each other's arms and sing a love duet whose simple tune sounds like a folk song. In a most marvelous manner Strauss suddenly makes this melodic line emerge as expressive of the simple, uncomplicated union of two human beings who love and fulfill one another.

The Marschallin, however, returns once more, this time accompanied by Sophie's father, who seems dumb struck by the kindness and benevolence the Marschallin has seen fit to bestow on him. Tenderly he embraces his daughter and then, with a great show of warmth, shakes the hand of his future son-in-law. "That's the way they are, these youngsters," he says, thoughtful and faintly amused, addressing the Marschallin. That, indeed, is the way they are, these youngsters—love and the future belong to them.

And sadly, with a smile of resignation, the Marschallin salutes them, acknowledging the rights of youth over her own claims to love. Aided by Faninal, she leaves the stage. Until now, firmly erect, every inch the duchess, she has not so much as glanced in the direction of Octavian; but now a single gesture of hers sums up all the generosity and warmth of her essential being. She holds out her hand, and Octavian kisses it with fervent gratitude. "Don't worry," the gesture is meant to convey. "I understand. And I have already forgiven."

She then disappears along with Faninal, leaving the two youngsters alone.

After a brief duet that repeats the folk-song motif, Octavian and Sophie also exit, and for an instant the stage remains empty.

But neither Strauss nor Hofmannsthal wanted this opera to end on a sentimental note; the delightful comedy had to have a touch of humor as its final moment. And so the little Moor, the Marschallin's attendant, comes prancing into the room. Sophie, it appears, has lost her handkerchief, and he looks around for it everywhere. Then, having found it at last, he waves it triumphantly and rushes off.

The curtain drops.

Postscript

*T*HESE FIVE STRAUSS operas in which I was chosen to sing the main roles comprise but a small part of my very extensive opera repertoire, but they always have loomed as milestones. And among them, in turn, the Marschallin stands out by herself. Long after I had given up most of my other roles in obedience to the inexorable command of time, I still was being recalled to the stage to re-create this, my favorite role. And whenever I sang it, I felt caught up in the sheer joy of it, swept away by its magic, the words and music streaming out as though they truly were part of myself and created by me. And whenever I closed the door on Sophie and Octavian to leave them to their bliss, I always felt as though I were closing the door upon part of my own life, taking leave with a smile.

But wasn't there a measure of reality in this feeling born out of the action on the stage? Every performance was, after all, a good-bye of sorts. Gradually I had become a guest in the bizarre and colorful world of the stage and I began to look about me as though I were a stranger there. And yet, when the final curtain did fall at last, it came as something of a surprise.

I had hoped to stay on with the Metropolitan on the basis of a few evenings during the season, feeling that I no longer could assume the obligations implicit in a long-term contract such as that proposed by the opera management. My offer was based not on caprice, but on realistic self-appraisal, which made it obvious to me that my vocal strength was no longer up to the grueling demands of a long opera season. The Metropolitan, however, remained adamant, and thus in 1946 I sang the Marschallin for the last time. Rumors of my impending retirement had got around, and the audience made this parting performance an experience both exceedingly difficult and overwhelmingly beautiful.

The curtain descended upon what to me was the greatest happiness in life.

But I am not one to sit back and do nothing. Life must be lived in all its many-faceted beauty, and new realms of adventure always are beckoning. Thus, after my retirement from the opera, I entered upon a new career as a Lieder singer that was to eclipse my previous one on the stage, discovered a new world that revealed to me new joys and a profound sense of accomplishment. The glamour of the stage receded into memories as I grew into my new role.

But once again there came the time to accept the inevitable, and in 1951 I quit the concert stage—once again at the right moment, when my faithful, beloved audience still did not want to let me go. But I knew better.

And strangely enough, as I at last retired into the sanctuary of a private individual, the joys and satisfactions I had experienced as a Lieder singer suddenly paled before the happy memories of the opera, the one world that truly had been my very own. Everything else, as I came to realize, was a substitute.

I remember an afternoon when, as I was lying under a flowering mimosa in our garden, someone turned on the radio in the house, and the bewitching strains of *Der Rosenkavalier* gripped my heart in an agonizing fit of despair. I realized that I had lost my world, but that I was not cut out to be sitting around to mourn the glories of the past. I needed to go on creating, working, being active.

Thus I ultimately found my way into teaching. Through my young students I once again could experience what had been the very essence of my being, and passing on to them what I had once acquired for myself thenceforth became my highest goal and purpose.

For me there now are no new worlds to conquer; but as I left the living experience, the glamour and turmoil of opera and concert stage behind me, I for the first time had the leisure and serenity to open my eyes to other forms of beauty, to see nature at long last instead of merely passing through it mindless of its glory, and to delve into the magic and mystery of art in fields other than music. Life is infinite in its wealth and variety; one must take hold of it. "Take your fill of life; we all go through it, yet how few come to know it. Wherever you take hold of it, the fascination is boundless."

How true; our task is to seek and discover life's infinite variety. Once upon a time I had devoted myself exclusively to the theater, whereas now I am part of the whole world, and therefore so much richer in my understanding of aspects that had once been alien and remote, rich in the knowledge that there is no end to the joy of learning and that one closes doors only in order to open new and different ones and that the miracle of change goes on forever.

Second Postcript

Der Rosenkavalier's enormous and continuing significance in my life was underscored by the invitation I received from the Metropolitan Opera to direct a performance of the opera. The idea originated with Constance Hope, my former publicity manager and faithful friend; Messrs. Bing and Gutman accepted the suggestion enthusiastically, but at first I turned it down. I was prevailed upon to change my mind only after I learned that Director Ralph Herbert would assist me, taking charge of details, such as the stage arrangements, which might prove to be beyond my strength.

A cable was dispatched to Paris asking Régine Crespin, the new Marschallin, to state frankly and truthfully how she would feel about working with me. The reply came back promptly; it would, she declared, be an artistic experience of the highest order.

Thus my reluctance was overcome, and I finally agreed. The remaining traces of hesitation were, I believe, more than understandable; there is an enormous difference between staging an opera with semiprofessional young singers at the Music

Academy of the West and handling a production at the Metropolitan. The cast here consisted of world-famous stars who had
sung in *Der Rosenkavalier* with regularity and great success
and who brought to their respective roles mature conceptions
of their own. It would have been against all my artistic prin-
ciples for me to try to change their ideas in any fundamental
way, even though I personally may not always agree with
them. I realized that the greatest possible tact would be imperative if I wished to succeed in making some of the correc-
tions and improvements I would perhaps regard as necessary.

However, my apprehensions proved unwarranted, for I encountered a truly moving cooperative and open-minded spirit
on the part of the entire cast, God bless them all, and thus in
the late autumn of life experienced the unique joy of a three-
fold rebirth.

My main concern was with the three major roles. Baron
Ochs was sung by Otto Edelmann in so expert a fashion that
there remained nothing for me to suggest. His conception of
the role was somewhat more robust than that of the unforgettable Richard Mayr, with whom I had sung it so many times
in Vienna and in London; Mayr's Viennese charm was truly
unique, and I shall never forget his *"Hier sitzt mit seiner Aller-
schoensten ein Verliebter beim Souper. . . ."* ("This is a lover,
dining here with his most charming girl"). He was at one and
the same time both nobleman and peasant, a perhaps inimitable
combination. Edelmann acted out a sharply etched portrait of
a peasant aristocrat, uncouth and shameless in his greed.

Sophie, as sung by Anneliese Rothenberger of the Vienna
Opera, was a charming creature, both tender and innocent,
truculent and temperamental, fighting with true Viennese
passion for her love and for her rights. Elisabeth Schumann,
my own beloved Sophie through so many years, used to lend
more emphasis to the shy reticence of a girl just emerged

from convent school, a pristine innocence that like a silver halo hovered above her delightful dark curls.

But Anneliese Rothenberger's Sophie warrants comparison with that of her famous predecessor, and by her different approach she reaffirms the essential vitality of the character in its manifold potentialities.

Octavian, as sung by Hertha Toepper of the Munich State Opera, could have been perfect if only she had come to see him my way as a radiant creature, a startlingly delightful young boy who does not grow up and change into a real man until the second act, when he sees himself cast in the role of Sophie's protector. Hertha, a beautiful woman, looked particularly dazzling in the second act, resplendent in her white-and-silver costume, and I do not want to be misunderstood: she was an excellent Octavian. Missing, however, in my opinion, was that final touch of irresistible charm. In the beginning she seemed to be fighting rather than trusting me, and it was not always easy to obtain her agreement. For that matter, given my basic orientation, I could not possibly have construed her conception as being "wrong" simply because it happened to differ from my own. Right is whatever one honestly feels. Hertha's Octavian proved to be a great success, and that is important. However, I happened to know how Strauss himself conceived of Octavian, and I saw him through Strauss's eyes.

But a gift not welcome is a useless gift.

Régine Crespin was a magnificent Marschallin. Never did I hear the beginning of the trio in the last act sung so divinely, with the most tender of pianissimos, almost unearthly in its silvery beauty. Perhaps my help proved valuable to Régine. In the beginning she seemed rather "French," full of charm and grace, perfectly delightful except that the character she was supposed to represent happened to be Viennese; and by God, it was a typical Viennese woman who sang the premiere. To work with that great artist was sheer joy from beginning to end, and I venture to believe that my feelings of profound personal friendship for her are mutual. My own Marschallin may have been somewhat less sentimental in the first act, but this genuinely felt sentimentality is part of Régine's being and should not be tampered with.

And I never shall forget Ralph Herbert and his prodigious labors in surmounting the many difficulties that arose. Many of the singers in the minor roles were new to them, and Ralph had to direct simultaneously the chorus and the soloists, a task of which he acquitted himself brilliantly, but with many a groan and sigh. His fits of utter despair—and I do hope he'll forgive this confession—struck me at times as outrageously funny. Somehow I had been through it all much too often to despair of the ultimate outcome. Many times I had seen proof of the old adage according to which poor rehearsals practically guarantee a successful premiere. This is a tradition in show business, and I still remember Director Loewenfeld in Hamburg pouncing on any opportunity for a temper tantrum that would enable him to walk out on a rehearsal and threaten to cancel the opening. If no opportunity presented itself, he would manufacture one. He never once disappointed us.

There were, of course, the usual number of incidents and calamities during the New York rehearsals. An undercover feud developed between Mr. Bing and Mr. Herbert about Octavian's entrance in the second act, with Mr. Bing wanting him to arrive in a stately coach. In itself maybe a rather good idea, except that according to the libretto this coach was to be drawn by six white horses, while all we had at our disposal were two fat old nags. Ralph Herbert implored me to support his opposition to this unfortunate vehicle, and when I agreed, he triumphantly confronted Mr. Bing, who promptly called me in and argued his side of the case. He really seemed attached to the idea of a coach, and as it would in any case be visible for only a moment, I did not see why one had to disappoint him. Thus we ended up with a coach and two horses.

Incidentally, it turned out rather a handsome sight at that, the two old animals decked out with tufts of ornamental plumes that failed to shake their well-tried equanimity.

Another funny episode concerned a meeting with my former colleague, Maria Jeritza, with whom I taped an interview for the broadcast of *Ariadne*. Jeritza had sung *Ariadne* at the Vienna premiere, at which I sang the Composer; it therefore seemed pertinent for the interviewer to ask us some questions concerning that first performance. Unfortunately, however, we both must have sounded rather foolish in our replies, for the memories we shared made us laugh and giggle constantly until the actual purpose of the interview became completely submerged by our unseemly high spirits. Several times I made futile attempts to formulate my answers on a more appropriately exalted intellectual level, but they invariably ended in chaotic frivolity. In the most amiable fashion, Maria and I exchanged remarks that in our youth would have been cause for blistering hostility or open battle; in retrospect, those rivalries of the past all seemed childish and unimportant.

Maria Jeritza still is a striking-looking woman, her hair still blond, her face—or as much of it as is visible behind the brim of that huge hat of hers and the dark glasses she affects—retains its former fresh vigor. She wears her hair as she always did, and her mouth has not yet unlearned its laughter. Next to her I felt a thousand years old.

It was indeed a gay hour; we even were served champagne, which I sipped with delight while Maria, in an astonishing display of abstemiousness, confined herself to ginger ale. Which, perhaps, was all to the good, for there is no way of telling what she would have said or done if the champagne had gone to her head.

For the first act of *Der Rosenkavalier,* a petshop delivered a charming gray poodle that I would have been happy to take with me. In fact, I was greatly tempted to inquire about the price, but we already own four dogs and really have no room for a fifth one. The pet dealer appeared onstage with a monkey sitting on his shoulder and carrying a frightened bird in a cage. Being a quasipathological lover of animals, I immediately appealed to Mr. Bing, who shares my concern for animals and who arranged for a stuffed bird to take the place of the live one.

A much less happy circumstance was the shortage of taxicabs in New York. The city is dreadfully overcrowded, and the Metropolitan Opera House is located right in the heart of it. Stepping out into Broadway at rush hour is to take one's life into one's hands. With almost unbelievable rudeness the crowds in New York will shove you right off the sidewalk into the street, where you run into immediate danger of being caught or impaled upon the bumpers of thousands of cars and cabs—the latter, however, all occupied. Used as I was to the divine quiet of Santa Barbara, I found it most difficult to adjust to that sort of existence. I often spent as much as half an hour waiting for a cab, desperately hailing anything in sight. To rent a car would have made no sense because parking is incredibly difficult, though I have since learned of a parking lot near the Metropolitan that might have solved my problem.

At the corner of Broadway and 39th Street was a newsstand guarded by a beautiful dog that I would stroke every time I passed; once this stand became a veritable refuge to me because I felt so desperately tired that I had to ask the vendor if he would let me sit with him for a few minutes. And there I sat, miserable, thinking of all the glamour and glory of an artist's life.

Otto Edelmann just happened to be passing at that moment,

and, in order to attract his attention, I sang a phrase from the second act of *Der Rosenkavalier*. "Here I lie . . ."

Startled, he looked up. "For heaven's sake, what are you doing here?"

"Waiting for a cab."

His efforts proved equally unavailing, and I ended up walking back to my hotel.

However, if you do manage to grab a cab, it often turns out to be a marvelous experience. The driver always starts the conversation going right away. There is one in particular whom I shall never forget. When told that I came from faraway California, he instantly informed me that all good-looking people invariably came from there. We then started talking, progress in New York traffic being what it is, and I told him that the city's street noises proved so distracting to me that I sometimes had to take a sleeping pill in order to get a good night's sleep. This bit of information so upset the poor fellow that we almost had an accident. Then he proceeded to give me a sternly paternal lecture. "Now you listen to me," he began. "Next time, just before you go to sleep, you take a glass of cold water. No ice in it—just cold tap water; ice upsets the stomach. You drink that water very, very slowly. And then—have you ever heard of self-hypnosis? Well, you say to yourself, 'I'm tired; I'm tired, and I am about to go to sleep. I feel myself falling asleep.' " I was genuinely moved by this expression of solicitude on his part; and when I left, I still heard him calling after me: "And no more pills, you hear? You gotta promise . . ."

I promised. And I actually tried his method—and found that it worked.

Thus my stay in New York came to an end. Many friends helped to make it a truly delightful one, and I am most grateful to them all.

Among the many flowers sent me at the first performance

of *Der Rosenkavalier* was a single silver rose. To this day I do not know the identity of the imaginative sender; the card that came with it bore the legend "Because we cannot forget." This rose was placed in a special vase, and when it opened two days later, the natural dark red of the petals offset by the silver seemed to express a luminous affection.

And the feelings of the unknown sender found an echo in my grateful heart.

Index

Aagard-Oestvig, Karl, 20–21, 33, 48
Alwin, Karl, 72
Arabella, Strauss, 26, 91–117:
 synopsis, 95–117
Ariadne auf Naxos, Strauss, 1–12,
 13–22, 111, 203:
 legend, 4
 synopsis, 6–12, 13–17, 19–20

Beecham, Sir Thomas, 169, 170
Bing, Rudolph, 199, 202, 204
Birkmayer, Toni, 56
Bourgeois Gentilhomme, Le, Mo-
 lière, 6
Brandes, Helene, 120
Brecher, Gustav, 119, 120
Busch, Fritz, 73–74

Correck, Joseph, 75
Covent Garden Opera, 120, 169
Crespin, Régine, 199, 201–202
Cumberland, Duke of, 24

Dresden, 71, 72, 73, 91
Dresden Opera, 71, 77

Duhan, Hans, 21

Edelmann, Otto, 200, 204

Fleischer-Edel, Editha, 119
Frau ohne Schatten, Die, Strauss:
 23–70
 libretto, 31, 63
 music, 63
 staging, 43–44, 55–56, 63
 synopsis, 32–48, 51–58, 59–63, 64–
 66, 67–70

Garmisch, Germany, 26
Gmunden, Austria, 23–24, 25
Gregor, Hans, 4, 5
Gutheil-Schoder, Marie, 2, 3, 5, 48

Hamburg, 2, 3, 119, 120
Hamburg Municipal Theater, 1
Herbert, Ralph, 199, 202
Hofmannsthal, Hugo von, 3, 6, 7,
 32, 55, 74, 109, 111, 123, 132,
 178, 194
Holgate, Ronald, 102

Hope, Constance, 199
Horenstein, Jascha, 26

Intermezzo, Strauss, 28, 71–89:
  libretto, 71, 74–75
  staging, 77–79, 86–87
  synopsis, 76–88

Jerger, Alfred, 87, 102, 115
Jeritza, Maria, 2, 21, 25, 48, 59, 66, 68, 153–54, 203

Klemperer, Otto, 120
Környey, Béla von, 20
Krauss, Clemens, 49–51, 91–92
Kurz, Selma, 2, 21

Lehmann, Lotte:
  in *Arabella*
    as Arabella, 92–93, 99, 107, 115
  in *Ariadne auf Naxos*
    as Ariadne, 5
    as the Composer, 3–5, 6, 17, 23, 203
    as Echo, 3
  in *Die Frau ohne Schatten*
    as the Dyer's Wife, 25, 39, 43–44, 48–49, 59, 63, 64
  directs Der Rosenkavalier, 199–206
  in *Intermezzo*
    as Christine, 72–75, 77
    as a lieder singer, 196
  in *Die Meistersinger*
    as Eva, 40
  in *Der Rosenkavalier*
    as the Marschallin, 120 *et seq.*
    as Octavian, 45, 120, 135
    as Sophie, 120
  in *Tannhäuser*
    as Elisabeth, 41
Lemnitz, Tiana, 169
Lohfing, Max, 119

Maikl, Georg, 21
Manowarda, Josef von, 49
Mayr, Richard, 2, 48, 64, 121, 135, 177, 200
Meistersinger von Nürnberg, Die, Wagner, 40
Metropolitan Opera, 148, 196, 199–200
Music Academy of the West, Santa Barbara, 102, 199–200
Muzzarelli, Alfred, 171–72

New York, 40

Opera buffa, 6

Paalen, Bella, 48, 67, 171

Reinhardt, Delia, 121
Roller, Alfred, 20, 21, 48
Rosenkavalier, Der, Strauss; 45, 110, 119–94, 197, 199, 200:
  libretto, 110–11, 119
  staging, 123–24, 147–48, 151, 152–53, 165, 202–203, 204
  synopsis, 123–51, 156–69, 172–94
Rothenberger, Anneliese, 200, 201
Royal and Imperial Court Opera, Vienna, 1; *see also* Vienna Opera
Rünger, Gertrud, 49

Salzburg Festival (1932), 63
Schalk, Franz, 2, 4, 18, 20, 24, 25, 49
Schubert, Franz, 16–17
Schuch, Lisl von, 77
Schumann, Elisabeth, 72, 119, 120, 121, 147, 173, 200
Sirota, Leo, 26
Strauss, Dr. Franz, 26, 82
Strauss, Pauline, 28–31, 50, 51, 74–75, 77, 78, 82, 83, 88, 89
Strauss, Richard, 3, 4, 5, 16–19, 25,

Strauss, Richard (*Cont.*):
26, 27–31, 39–40, 44, 49, 50, 51,
59, 67, 71, 72–75, 77, 81, 82, 83,
88, 89, 91, 92, 115, 124, 156, 164,
194, 201:
lieder, 30
operas, *see Arabella, Ariadne auf
Naxos, Die Frau ohne Schatten, Intermezzo,* and *Der
Rosenkavalier*

Tannhäuser, Wagner, 40
Toepper, Hertha, 201
Toscanini, Arturo, 40, 92, 156

Ursuleac, Viorica, 49, 91, 92, 115

Vienna, 1–2, 91, 92, 93, 102, 120
Vienna Opera, 2, 4, 5, 21, 22, 153,
171, 200
Völker, Franz, 49

Walker, Edyth, 119, 120
Wallerstein, Lothar, 50, 63–64, 154
Walter, Bruno, 40, 120, 155, 156
Weidt, Lucy, 2, 48
Wymetal, Wilhelm von, 2, 3, 20,
153, 154